KU-612-247

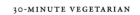

30-MINUTE VEGETARIAN

YLVA BERGQVIST

WATERFORD CITY AND COUNTY LIBRARIES WITHDRAWN

30 MINUTE VEGETARIAN

100 GREEN RECIPES TO MAKE IN 30 MINUTES OR LESS

hardie grant books

First published by © Bonnier Fakta 2017
The English language edition published in 2018 by Hardie Grant Books,
an imprint of Hardie Grant Publishing

Hardie Grant Books (London)
5th & 6th Floors
52–54 Southwark Street
London SE1 1UN

Hardie Grant Books (Melbourne)
Building 1, 658 Church Street
Richmond, Victoria 3121

hardiegrantbooks.com

All rights reserved. No part of this publication may be reproduced, stored in a
retrieval system or transmitted in any form by any means, electronic, mechanical,
photocopying, recording or otherwise, without the prior written permission of
the publishers and copyright holders.

The moral rights of the author have been asserted.

Text © Ylva Bergqvist 2017
Photography © Lennart Weibull 2017

British Library Cataloguing-in-Publication Data. A catalogue record for this
book is available from the British Library.

30-Minute Vegetarian by Ylva Bergqvist

ISBN 978-1-78488-186-3

Graphic Design: Lukas Möllersten
Editor: Susanna Eriksson Lundqvist
Layout: jk morris production AB, Värnamo

For the English hardback edition:

LEABHARLANN PHORT LÁIRGE	
Bertrams	23/10/2018
UA	02361192

Live life a little greener

More vegetables and less or no meat at all – that's how more and more people are eating today. The reason why varies, but almost everyone agrees that mum was right when she said that vegetables are healthy and good for you. Most would probably agree that a vegetarian diet is better for the environment. I would also like to add that it is delicious.

Perhaps you're already a vegetarian or vegan looking for new inspiration for your weekday meals – after all, it's a weekday 260 days of the year. Or perhaps you're like me – a meat eater with green ambitions.

I eat vegetarian at lunchtime and make meat-free soups on Mondays. If it were up to me, my family would eat vegetarian daily. I'm trying to get my unaccustomed children used to vegan pizzas, lentil pancakes and tacos with nuts and beans. I also sneak in the vegetables by serving a salad as a starter, in the form of a fillings for sandwiches or by serving extra vegetables on the dinner table.

I think it's easier to start living life greener if you can put food on the table quickly. That's why all the dishes in this book take around half an hour to prepare. Some have to be put in the oven so the full cooking time amounts to over an hour, but while the food cooks you can do something nice like read a book. Half the recipes are vegan, which means they are made using solely plant-based ingredients. They're marked with this symbol: ⊕. The rest are lacto-ovo vegetarian, so may include both eggs and dairy products. Where it's possible, there are tips on how to make recipes completely plant-based. The book also includes basic recipes for things like kimchi, falafel and paneer; ingredients that take longer to make but which are better and cheaper if you make them yourself.

I've taken inspiration for the recipes from around the world, and hopefully they will encourage you to live life greener right here on your own home turf. Above all, I would love to be a fly on the wall in your kitchen to see what you're cooking. Feel free to post on social media using the hashtag #30minutevegetarian or #100greens so that I can follow your green life. I promise to tag my own dishes so that we can inspire each other.

A GOOD START

When you've decided which dish you want to make and have bought all the ingredients, all you have to do is wash your hands, roll up your sleeves and get started. Here are few tips to make it go like clockwork.

Read the recipe!

The old adage that you should read the recipe from beginning to end before you start cooking is from back in the mists of time, but it's still applicable today. What if you don't have an oven in your kitchen and you discover halfway through that the vegetables are supposed to be roasted . . . OK, so that's not the best example, but you get the point.

Get out all the ingredients

Before you starting cooking, it's good to get out all the ingredients. If there's anything missing, you can skip it or be creative and search your larder for an exciting substitute. Consider it an opportunity. That's how new recipes and flavour combinations are most frequently created.

Get out your tools

A carpenter has screwdrivers on a belt or in a toolbox nearby. You don't need to buy a belt, even if that would be cool, but do make sure you get out all the tools and equipment you will need before starting. Chopping board, knife, peeler, measures, grater, bowls, frying pan (skillet) and saucepan, etc. You'll save time and avoid having to wipe messy fingerprints off your kitchen cupboards.

Use the right equipment

To save time and avoid frustration, it's important to have the right tools. A good, coarse grater and a sharp, fine grater (for example, a microplane grater for zesting lemons and grating ginger) are both important. Two good frying pans (skillets) are useful because it means you can fry two things at once. At least one of them should have a lid.

I like my mandolin, which allows me to slice things thinly, but a cheese slicer is also fine. A really good potato peeler is worth its weight in gold, as is a pair of scissors to cut up herbs and spring onions (scallions). A hand-held blender and a food processor are two other great pieces of kit to have. Yet, most important of all is having sharp knives!

Measure by eye and use known measures

If you want to become a better cook and work more quickly in the kitchen, you can try measuring by eye and using your tastebuds instead of teaspoons and tablespoons for spices, salt and sugar. Practise by pouring a measured teaspoon or tablespoon of sugar onto a white plate or into the palm of your hand to train your eye to learn how much it is.

Season a little at a time, and taste often. Be very cautious with chilli, salt and sugar. Too much sugar can be adjusted with a little acid. Too much chilli or salt is trickier to deal with, but you can often dilute with a little extra liquid.

I rarely use measures for lemon and lime juice. I know that a squeezed lime gives around 2 tablespoons of juice and a lemon around 3. If I squeeze a particularly large or a small and dry citrus fruit, I adjust my amounts accordingly. I prefer to peel ginger using a small teaspoon. Then I grate it finely and squeeze out the juice. All the flavour is in the juice, while the dry core is mostly fibre. A piece of ginger weighing 40 g (1½ oz) provides around 1 tablespoon of ginger juice. Since all roots look different, it's difficult to have an exact measure for what 40 g looks like, but it's about the same as a thumb.

Set up a compost bin and preparation space

I usually put a large bowl in the sink or on the counter for compost and another for any other rubbish, which saves me having to run to the bin all the time.

Prepare a space near the cooker where you can stand and chop or stir while also keeping an eye on what's going on in the frying pans (skillets) and saucepans.

Use oven heat

When you're baking something – cakes, pizza, bread, pies – it's important to put it into a preheated oven as the temperature needs to be even. When I'm roasting root vegetables, tomatoes, potatoes or making other vegetable dishes, it's fine to put the tray into a cold oven and save time and energy.

It's difficult to provide the exact time something needs to spend in the oven, but check the food and add time if it isn't done. Feel free to open the oven door and move things around a few times. Most oven dishes are actually improved if you open the door and let a little steam out every now and then.

Know your onions

Fried onions are the basis of almost all cookery, but they are easily burnt if they're not given proper attention. I often start by frying the chopped onion in quite a lot of fat over a low-medium heat. The onion can then simmer away as I prepare the next step. When my hands are free again, I stir it and turn up the temperature and carry on frying.

I peel garlic cloves by pressing the palm of my hand against the broad side of a knife so that they are crushed and the peel comes off. This saves frustration and time. Since I think finely chopped garlic tastes better than pressed garlic, I always chop it. If you're really up against it, though, you can always save time by using a garlic press.

Take shortcuts

If you have an induction or gas hob, you can boil water quickly. If your hob is slower, it is quick and more energy-efficient to boil water in a kettle first. Do you have a food processor gathering dust? Use it! After all, it saves you valuable time.

Symbols in the book

Dishes marked with this symbol are vegan, which means they only contain plant-based ingredients.	Tips for other tasty dishes if you have leftovers after cooking the main recipe.

A VARIED DIET

Just like meat and fish eaters, vegetable lovers need to get all their nutrients. As long as you don't think that sweets are a crucial part of your diet, you don't need to worry. You also don't need to think about ensuring every meal is complete. The important thing is to eat a varied diet.

Protein forms the body's building blocks and is needed for both cells and muscles. If you eat meat, it's pretty straightforward – all you do is consume ingredients that once walked or swam and you're sorted. If you only eat vegetables, you need to adopt a new reminder: eat a healthy and varied diet and you will get enough protein.

There's protein in practically all food. You find it in cabbage, oats, flour and mushrooms, to name just a few of the rather more unexpected ingredients. The real heavyweights are beans, peas and lentils, as well as products made from these, such as tofu, miso and soy milk. Quinoa, buckwheat, flaxseed and nuts are also great features on your plate when it comes to protein. It's also a good idea to select flour made from protein-rich ingredients, such as chickpea (gram) flour, almond flour and buckwheat flour.

If you're not a vegan and you're happy to eat eggs, cheese and dairy products, these are excellent sources of both protein and calcium. One of the most surprising sources of protein is actually cocoa.

You also consume enough vitamins and minerals – with two exceptions: vitamin B12 and iron. Vitamin B12 is mostly found in animal-based products such as meat, as well as in eggs and milk. If you're a vegetarian, and especially if you're vegan, the vitamin can be in short supply. You can drink B12-enriched vegetable drinks and a small quantity is also found in fermented food such as, kimchi and sauerkraut. To be on the safe side, you can also buy vitamin tablets or nutritional yeast from a health food shop. One and a half tablespoons of nutritional yeast provides your daily requirement of both B12 and other B vitamins, as well as a little extra umami. Stir a spoonful into sauces and sandwich fillings or make vegesan (vegan Parmesan). In other words, it's great for your body and your tastebuds.

Iron is found in lots of vegetables, such as soybeans, nuts, seeds, wholegrain flour, lentils, chickpeas (garbanzos) and kale. The problem is that the body needs a little assistance to absorb vegetable-based iron. You can help by eating or drinking something rich in vitamin C like a glass of orange juice or having some strawberries with your meal, as well as opting for wholewheat. If you germinate beans and lentils before cooking them, your body can more easily absorb the iron. Dried apricots are another good source of iron, so rounding off every meal with an apricot dipped in chocolate isn't a bad idea.

IN THE VEGGIE LOVER'S LARDER

*Here are my fourteen top ingredients and products that it's worth
having to hand so you can cook tasty, healthy vegetarian dishes.
Complement with seasonal fruit and vegetables.*

Pre-cooked beans and uncooked lentils

Beans are extremely rich in protein and easy to cook on their own. However, they take more than half an hour to prepare, which is why tinned beans are the saviour of cooks who don't plan ahead. If you want to live an egg-free life, then aquafaba (the Latin for water and beans) is perfect for using in things like gnocchi and mayonnaise.

My larder contains *lentils* – red, black and green – primarily dried ones. Lentils are healthy, protein-rich and quick to cook – they are ready in just half an hour. Home-cooked lentils are far tastier than tinned ones, but long-life green lentils can be used if necessary. I usually avoid the red ones as the colour is off, they are mushy and have an unwelcome aftertaste.

Frozen greens

Peas, soybeans, edamame beans (soybeans still in their pods), *haricots verts* and *kale* are great dinner savers to pull out of the freezer when the veggie box is empty. Put peas in a creamy pasta, use soybeans for fried rice, fry haricots verts with garlic and lemon, steam edamame beans or make a kale omelette. The list goes on . . .

My freezer also contains whole lemongrass, whole kaffir lime leaves, whole chillies and grated ginger. They're wonderful for adding flavour and can be frozen, which is great as you can't always find kaffir lime leaves and lemongrass in the supermarket. Robust herbs like parsley, thyme and rosemary can also withstand being frozen. Pomegranate seeds and mango are available to buy frozen. You don't have to peel, deseed or dice, and they are always ripe.

Stock, miso and nutritional yeast

Umami is a flavour, just like sweet and salty. Usually, we say that umami provides 'depth' and 'body' to dishes, and the flavour is found in many foods – from breast milk (!) to Parmesan, tomatoes and stock. I buy ready-made liquid stock and usually have a vegetable stock and a chanterelle stock at home.

Umami is also found in miso (fermented soybean paste). There are several kinds, but I usually buy white miso (shiro miso). A small spoon of this marvel is well worth trying any time you think your dinner didn't turn into the masterpiece you had hoped for.

Nutritional yeast also provides the umami flavour, as well as vital vitamin B for your body. This yeast can be found in health food shops. Both miso and nutritional yeast can be omitted from most recipes, although doing so would be a shame since they make your food not only tastier but also healthier.

Fermented vegetables

In Korea, they're crazy about fermented vegetables and the best known pickle is probably *kimchi* – fermented cabbage. Closer to home, cabbage is fermented without chilli and is known as *sauerkraut*. All fermented and sour creamed vegetables are very healthy and contain small quantities of vitamin B12. You can buy sour creamed vegetables, and sometimes even kimchi, in normal shops. If you want to make your own kimchi, there is a recipe on page 173.

Asian flavourings

Every now and then, I go to Asian stores and fill my basket with flavourings for the larder. Apart from *white miso*, I buy *Japanese* (light) soy sauce, the sweet Indonesian soy sauce *ketjap manis*, the sweet Chinese *hoisin sauce*, the Thai chilli sauce *sriracha*, the Japanese dried seasoning *furikake*, the Chinese spice blend five spice and the Japanese breadcrumb *panko*.

I also buy *coconut cream*. It's creamier and much tastier than coconut milk, which is really just diluted coconut cream. In the shop, I usually ask which sesame oil they think is best, and then I buy the most expensive. This is because bad sesame oil tastes like burnt rubber, and isn't especially nice in food.

Sometimes, I buy *black chilli bean paste*, dried *shiitake mushrooms* for rich stocks and Korean *gochugaru* (Korean chilli powder) for kimchi. Some of these ingredients are sold in supermarkets, but they are usually of a better quality and cheaper in Asian stores.

Ripe tomatoes

For a few months a year, fresh tomatoes are both cheap and delicious. When that's the case, gorge yourself on them. Occasionally, if you're flashing the cash, you might want to buy *romantica* tomatoes. They are almost always sweet, regardless of the time of year.

The rest of the time, I suggest you buy tinned tomatoes. As it doesn't say on the tin which kind of tomatoes are inside, you will have to keep trying them until you find your favourite, or buy the most expensive one. Price and quality are usually related. There is one kind that is named on the tin. They are whole San Marzano tomatoes. They grow in sight of Vesuvius, are a little sweeter and less acidic than other types, and definitely worth the extra premium.

Nuts, almonds and seeds

I love sprinkling *nuts*, *almonds* and *seeds* on food; if it was up to me, they would be on the top of every dish out there. This is mostly because I love the taste and the crispiness, but also because it's healthy. Nuts, almonds and seeds contain a lot of protein, and many vitamins and minerals. The slight downside is that they are a little fatty, even if this is healthy fat. The fat means that they can easily go rancid, but a smart trick is to put them in the freezer – you don't even have to defrost them before use. Peanuts and cashews are usually available in large packs in Asian stores at low prices.

All nuts, almonds and seeds taste better if toasted in a dry pan before use. Do this if you have the time.

Rice, grains and flour

Different rices and grains are worth having to hand to quickly be able to throw together a filling dinner. Do with rice as you do with everything else in your life: buy the one you love – *wholegrain rice* or *brown rice* or the polished ones like *jasmine* or *basmati*.

Bulgur, *couscous* and *rye* are grains made using wheat. *Polenta (cornmeal)* is made with crushed corn kernels, and is largely used for porridge, but you can also use it to coat vegetables. You can also buy the protein-rich grain *quinoa* or *buckwheat* or, from less far afield, grains like *edible barley* or *edible oats*.

Both *almond flour* and *chickpea (gram) flour* are protein-rich types of flour that are perfect for patties and pancakes.

Pasta

Nowadays, there are many types of *pasta* to choose from, including those that aren't made from wheat. The recipes simply state that you should use pasta, but the choice is then yours. If you're vegan, you should obviously use egg-free pasta. Why not try a gluten-free and protein-rich pasta made using buckwheat, beans, quinoa or millet? You can also use a slightly healthier version of standard wheat-based pasta, such as one made using wholegrain flour.

Eggs, cheese and milk

If you don't eat conventional dairy products, there are many good plant-based alternatives made using soy, almonds and oats, but if you are willing to eat eggs, cheese and milk from cows, sheep or goats, then I think you should. They're both healthy and useful.

Eggs are probably the first ingredient I would take with me to a desert island. You may not be able to grow eggs, but they contain lots of protein and all the vitamins and minerals a person requires, apart from vitamin C.

Cheese and dairy products contain lots of protein, as well as calcium and vitamin K. There is a warning when it comes to cheese, though. Some lacto-ovo vegetarians don't eat cheese because many cheeses are made with rennet, an enzyme extracted from a calf's stomach. The quantity of rennet is very small, but if it says it contains rennet, then that is an animal product.

Vegetable rennet exists, which is known as 'vegetable/microbial curdling enzyme' or 'milk coagulant enzyme'. If it says this on the packaging, then the cheese is appropriate for strict lacto-ovo vegetarians to eat.

Paneer

In India, the cow is a holy animal, but that doesn't stop her from producing a lot of delicious milk. Over the years, the Indians have therefore become very talented at using and inventing products based on milk, including ghee (clarified butter), yoghurt and the fresh cheese *paneer*.

If you live in a bigger town, you can find paneer in Asian supermarkets, usually in the freezer, but it's easy to make yourself. It does require strong arms (you have to carry a few litres of milk home) and planning, as it takes a while before the cheese is ready. Make a big batch and freeze it. Instead of paneer, you can use halloumi. It's not the same thing, but it also tastes good.

12
Tofu

Tofu – soybean curd – was invented in China around two thousand years ago, is rich in protein and good to eat when you can't stand to see another bean. The softest type is known as silken tofu, and, as the name implies, it is soft and silky smooth. It's best crumbled, for instance into a soup or a wok. You can also whisk it to make ice cream and various kinds of baked goods.

Firm tofu is good for flash-frying, deep-frying or using in casseroles. Some describe tofu as insipid, but useful is a more pleasant way of putting it since it absorbs lots of flavour. You can buy it natural, marinated or smoked. It's easy to marinate it at home, but smoking it is a little more challenging.

13
Oil and butter

The ingredients lists in this book feature both butter and various oils. I mostly use butter because of the flavour. If you are vegan, there is no good substitute available, but oil and margarine can be used for frying. I use various oils in the recipes, including sometimes in the same recipe, which is because they have different characteristics. Hot-pressed oils, usually referred to as neutral, can be used for frying, while cold-pressed oils shouldn't be heated up.

Hot-pressed *rapeseed (canola) oil* can be heated to high temperatures and contains lots of the healthy fatty acid omega-3. Hot-pressed *olive oil* contains more omega-6 and more flavour, and is suitable for roasting but not frying.

Cold-pressed rapeseed (canola) and olive oil are good for dressings, and add flavour to Mediterranean dishes. *Maize oil* and *sunflower oil* are not as healthy in terms of their fat content, while *peanut (ground-nut) oil*, which is a little more expensive and is produced far from Europe, is healthier.

Sometimes I use *sesame oil* for Asian cooking, but this isn't very good for frying. It's also quite dominant, which is why I usually mix it with a neutral-flavoured oil. Use it for dressings or as a flavouring after cooking.

14
Honey, sugar and sweeteners

A variety of sweeteners appear in the recipes. The sweetness lifts certain flavours and balances others, such as sour flavours. I state quantities in the recipes, but at certain times of year lemons are more acidic and tomatoes are sweeter, so it's best to taste your way to the right balance.

Set *honey* tastes better than liquid honey, but liquid honey is easier to use. Vegans can use *maple syrup* or agave syrup (made using the Mexican agave plant) as a sweetener. Agave syrup is sweeter and both are thinner in consistency than honey. Normal sugar is a cheap alternative suitable for all.

1

MEDITERRANEAN MAGIC

Creamy pasta dishes and other delicious meals from the Mediterranean

---

No fewer than 22 countries have shores on the Mediterranean, which means there is a whole sea to take inspiration from. We all know that Mediterranean food is not only tasty but also healthy. So gorge yourself on Italian pasta, Greek halloumi, North African spices, and hummus and falafel from the Middle East.

400 g (14 oz) egg-free
pasta, e.g. spaghetti

LENTIL BOLOGNESE

1 yellow onion, diced

1 carrot, peeled and diced

3 garlic cloves, finely chopped

1 teaspoon fennel seed

1 teaspoon dried rosemary

2 tablespoons tomato
purée (paste)

2 × 400 g (14 oz) tins
plum tomatoes

100 ml (3½ fl oz/½ cup)
wine, red or white

2 tablespoons concentrated
vegetable stock

400 g (14 oz) tin cooked
green lentils, drained, or
300 g (10½ oz/1½ cups)
home-cooked lentils

sugar, salt and freshly
ground black pepper

olive oil, for frying

Pasta with lentil bolognese

When you feel like a really rich, foodie pasta dish, this is what to make. The sauce tastes best if you cook the lentils al dente in a separate saucepan, but if you're in a hurry then it's fine to use tinned lentils. It's worth remembering that 100 g (3½ oz/½ cup) of uncooked lentils turn into just under 300 g (10½ oz/1½ cups) after they are cooked. If you're a liquorice lover, you can double the fennel seeds in this recipe. Serve with panko and lemon sprinkles or vegesan (pages 178–179) and a green salad.

1. Bring a pan of salted water to the boil, or fill from the kettle.
2. Fry the onion in a little oil in a large frying pan (skillet) for around 5 minutes over a medium-low heat until soft.
3. Raise the heat and add the carrot, garlic, fennel, rosemary and tomato purée to the pan (skillet) and fry for 1 minute, stirring.
4. Pour in the tomatoes, wine and stock and leave to simmer for another 15 minutes.
5. In the meantime, cook the pasta in the boiling water following the instructions on the pack.
6. Stir the lentils into the sauce and leave to simmer for a few minutes. Season with sugar, salt and pepper.
7. Drain the pasta but save 100 ml (3½ fl oz/½ cup) of the water. Mix into the sauce then serve with the pasta.

SPAGHETTI PANCAKES

If you have spaghetti leftover, you can make pancakes the day after. Cut the spaghetti into smaller pieces. Whisk 1 egg for every 300 g (10½ oz) of pasta and stir in some grated mature cheese and approximately 75 ml (2½ fl oz/⅓ cup) single (light) cream in a bowl. Mix in the spaghetti. Season with salt and freshly ground black pepper to taste. Fry small pancakes in a frying pan (skillet) with butter or oil. Serve with tomato sauce.

Pasta with pea and pistachio pesto and eggs

For a few months every spring and early summer, it's asparagus season. Mark it in your calendar in big letters to make sure you get your fill. For the rest of the year, it's fine to use broccoli for this dish. Why not make a double batch of the pesto? It's good in salads or as a dipping sauce if mixed with a little yoghurt.

4 eggs

400 g (14 oz) pasta,
e.g. mafaldine

500 g (1 lb 2 oz) broccoli
or asparagus

pea sprouts, lime zest and
basil leaves, to garnish

PEA AND PISTACHIO PESTO

75 g (2½ oz) Parmesan,
finely grated

300 g (10½ oz) frozen green
peas (petits pois), defrosted

1 garlic clove, finely chopped

75 g (2½ oz/⅓ cup)
peeled pistachios

100 ml (3½ fl oz/½ cup) olive oil

1 tablespoon freshly
squeezed lime juice

salt and chilli flakes

VEGAN

**Make the pesto without
Parmesan and season
with nutritional yeast.
Leave out the eggs and
use egg-free pasta.**

1. Bring a pan of salted water to the boil, or fill from the kettle.
2. Mix the cheese with 200 g (7 oz) of the peas, the garlic and the rest of the pesto ingredients in a food processor. Season with salt and chilli flakes to taste.
3. Soft boil the eggs for 6–7 minutes. Rinse in cold water.
4. Cook the pasta in boiling water following the instructions on the pack.
5. If you are using broccoli, remove the stalk. Cut the whole broccoli into around six pieces along its length. If you are using asparagus, break off the tough lower part of the asparagus and cut the rest into small pieces.
6. Add the broccoli or asparagus when the pasta has 2 minutes left to cook.
7. Drain the pasta but save 100 ml (3½ fl oz/½ cup) of the reserved water. Mix the pasta, water, broccoli or asparagus, pesto and the rest of the peas.
8. Peel off the tops of the egg shells and spoon the contents over the pasta. Top with pea sprouts, lime zest and basil.

Pasta with carrot sauce and buttery hazelnuts

The 90s called and demanded I include a recipe for carrot sauce in the book. And why not? It's quick, tasty – and cheap. I have improved the recipe a little by using yoghurt instead of cream. I've also added buttery hazelnuts and sneaked in a little protein. Instead of chervil, you can use lovage or parsley. Just as green and just as delicious.

1. Bring a pan of salted water to the boil, or fill from the kettle.
2. To make the sauce, fry the onion and garlic in oil in a saucepan over a low heat for 5–10 minutes until soft.
3. Peel and coarsely grate three of the carrots in the meantime. Peel and cut the fourth one into long strips using the peeler.
4. Mix the grated carrots, tomatoes, beans and water in a saucepan. Add the stock (if you're using miso, wait to mix this in until the sauce has combined). Raise the heat and leave to cook for approximately 15 minutes until the carrots have softened.
5. Cook the pasta in the boiling water following the instructions on the pack.
6. Toast the hazelnuts in the butter in a frying pan (skillet).
7. Mix the carrot sauce until smooth using a hand-held blender or food processor. Stir in the miso if you are using it, and add honey, salt and pepper to taste.
8. Layer the carrot sauce and yoghurt with pasta on the plates. Pour the nuts over the plates and top with the carrot strips, chervil or salad leaves. Sprinkle chilli flakes on top if you want some extra heat.

SERVES 4

400 g (14 oz) pasta,
e.g. linguine

300 g (10½ oz/1¼ cups) yoghurt

chervil or a handful of small,
tender salad leaves and
chilli flakes, to garnish

CARROT SAUCE

1 yellow onion

2 garlic cloves, finely chopped

rapeseed (canola)
oil, for frying

4 medium carrots

400 g (14 oz) tin plum tomatoes

150 g (5 oz) cooked
butter (lima) beans

200 ml (7 fl oz/¾ cup) water

1 tablespoon of concentrated
vegetable stock or
1–2 tablespoons white miso

honey, salt, black pepper

BUTTERY HAZELNUTS

100 g (3½ oz/¾ cup) hazelnuts,
roughly chopped

50 g (2 oz) butter

VEGAN

Use egg-free pasta and dairy-free yoghurt. Choose agave syrup instead of honey and toast the nuts without butter.

PASTA WITH PEA
AND PISTACHIO
PESTO AND EGGS
(PAGE 20)

PASTA WITH CARROT
SAUCE AND BUTTERY
HAZELNUTS (PAGE 21)

Pasta with kale and avocado

SERVES 4

400 g (14 oz) egg-free
pasta, e.g. spaghetti

300 g (10½ oz) fresh kale

3 garlic cloves, finely sliced

½–1 chilli, finely sliced

100 g (3½ oz/¾ cup) walnuts

3 ripe avocados, mashed

salt and freshly ground
black pepper

olive oil, for frying

basil leaves, to garnish

vegesan (page 179), to serve

A few years ago, a recipe began to circulate online for pasta with avocado created by a smart Finnish blogger. Then kale came along and took the world by storm. Avocado is undeniably green, so why not let the two storm away together? If you eat cheese, you can serve the pasta with grated pecorino – sheep's cheese – or Parmesan instead of vegesan (page 179).

1. Bring a pan of salted water to the boil, or fill from the kettle. Cook the pasta following the instructions on the pack.
2. Remove the hard middle stalk of the kale and strip the rest off into smaller pieces.
3. Toast the walnuts in a frying pan (skillet) without any fat. When they have cooled slightly, roughly chop the nuts or crush with a mortice.
4. Fry the kale, garlic and chilli in oil for around 4 minutes until soft. Mix in the nuts and let them get warm.
5. Season the mashed avocado with salt and pepper.
6. Drain the pasta but keep about 100 ml (3½ fl oz/½ cup) of the water. Mix the pasta with the cooking water, kale and avocado mash. Season with salt and pepper, and garnish with basil leaves. Serve with plenty of vegesan.

PASTA WITH KALE
AND AVOCADO
(ABOVE)

Pasta with tomato sauce and brown caper butter

If there were a Nobel Prize for recipe creators, the inventor of fried capers would definitely be a prime candidate. They are fantastically delicious, especially with brown butter. If you're worried about protein, you could mix in some cooked chickpeas (garbanzos) or red lentils into the sauce, make the roasted chickpeas on page 144 and sprinkle them on top, or choose a protein-rich pasta. If you don't like capers or don't have the energy, you can just drop the butter into the tomato sauce. And if you're completely exhausted, it's fine to buy ready-made tomato sauce. Isn't life full of opportunities!

1. Bring a pan of salted water to the boil, or fill from the kettle. Cook the pasta following the instructions on the pack.
2. In another large saucepan, fry the onion in rapeseed oil for around 5 minutes over a medium-low heat until soft.
3. Add the garlic, rosemary and tomato purée and fry for a further minute. Add the tomatoes and simmer for around 10–15 minutes. Carefully break the tomatoes apart using a wooden spoon.
4. Brown the capers in a frying pan (skillet) with a knob of the butter until they open up like small flowers. Place them in a bowl. Put the rest of the butter in the frying pan and brown it until it smells nutty and is light brown in colour. Pour the butter over the capers.
5. Season the tomato sauce with miso, honey, salt and pepper to taste.
6. Drain the pasta but save approximately 100 ml (3½ fl oz/½ cup) of the water. Mix the pasta with the tomato sauce and the water you held back. Plate up the pasta and pour the caper butter on top. Grate over a generous amount of Parmesan and then sprinkle chopped parsley on top.

SERVES 4

400 g (14 oz) pasta,
e.g. rigatoni

**Parmesan and chopped
flat-leaf parsley, to serve**

TOMATO SAUCE

1 yellow onion, diced

2 garlic cloves, finely chopped

2 teaspoons dried rosemary

**1 tablespoon tomato
purée (paste)**

**2 × 400 g (14 oz) tins
plum tomatoes**

1–2 tablespoons white miso

honey

**salt and freshly ground
black pepper**

**rapeseed (canola)
oil, for frying**

BROWN CAPER BUTTER

4 tablespoons capers

75 g (2½ oz) butter

VEGAN

**Use egg-free pasta.
Round off the sauce using a
little dairy-free cream and
swap the honey for agave
syrup. Fry the capers in oil.
Serve with vegan cheese.**

Celeriac mash with brown sage butter and butter beans

What does it take to turn classic mashed potatoes into a delicious dish? Flirtation with Italy. Do you want even more inspiration for mash varieties? Use Jerusalem artichokes or cauliflower instead of celeriac and pour caper butter (page 24) on top. Big potatoes, a kettle and not waiting for the oven to get hot are three tricks that speed up cooking to make sure this meal is ready in half an hour.

SERVES 4

250 g (9 oz) celeriac (celery root), peeled and chopped

750 g (1 lb 10 oz) large floury potatoes, peeled and chopped

olive oil, for frying

salt and freshly ground black pepper

500 g (1 lb 2 oz) broccoli or broccolini

75 g (2½ oz) butter

big bunch of sage leaves

400 g (14 oz) tin butter (lima) beans, rinsed

200 ml (7 fl oz/¾ cup) milk or single (light) cream

50 g (2 oz) Parmesan, grated

Lemon-marinated red onion (page 152)

1. Preheat the oven to 220°C (430°F/Gas 8).
2. Bring a pan of salted water to the boil, or fill from the kettle. Boil the celeriac and potatoes until soft (around 15–20 minutes).
3. Divide the whole broccoli into six parts. Place the pieces on a baking tray lined with baking paper, pour some olive oil on top and season with salt. Put the tray in the oven and roast for 15 minutes. If the broccoli hasn't taken on enough colour, you can use the grill to finish it off for a further 5 minutes.
4. Brown the butter in a saucepan until it stops spluttering. Add the sage leaves and continue to cook until the butter is light brown and smells nutty, and the leaves are fried. Pour into a bowl to stop the browning. Add the beans to the bowl so that they warm up.
5. Drain the celeriac and potatoes and mash or whisk into a mash with the milk or cream. Season with salt and pepper.
6. Plate up the mash. Add the broccoli and spoon the sage butter and beans on top. Finish with the Parmesan. Serve with a side dish of lemon-marinated red onion.

BEAN BURGERS
WITH MASH

Save any leftover mash and mix with a whisked egg, grated flavourful cheese and mashed beans. Season with salt, pepper and chopped herbs. Form into patties and turn them in panko breadcrumbs. Fry the patties in oil until crispy.

Bean gnocchi with mushrooms and spinach

The recipe for this fantastic gnocchi is borrowed from my friend Maria. It's quick to make and contains no eggs, but it does feature lots of hidden proteins. If you don't like spinach and mushrooms, you can serve it with a tasty tomato sauce – why not the one with chilli and lemon on page 30? If you round it off with a knob of butter, it's even more delicious.

page 30

SERVES 4

2 × 400 g (14 oz) tins butter (lima) beans

90 g (3¼ oz/¾ cup) plain (all-purpose) flour

100 g (3½ oz/⅔ cup) finely ground polenta (cornmeal)

50 g (2 oz) butter, for frying

grated Parmesan, to serve

FRIED MUSHROOMS AND SPINACH

200 g (7 oz) mushrooms, sliced

olive oil, for frying

2 garlic cloves, finely sliced

200 g (7 oz) baby spinach

salt and freshly ground black pepper

FRIED TOMATOES

2 tomatoes, halved

olive oil, for frying

VEGAN

Skip the butter and use vegesan (page 179) instead of Parmesan.

page 179

1. Bring a pan of salted water to the boil, or fill from the kettle.
2. Drain the beans but save around 60 ml (2 fl oz/¼ cup) of the water. Mix the beans with the water. Add the plain flour and mix into a fairly firm mass. The water is usually salty, but taste it to be sure and add salt if necessary.
3. Pour out half of the polenta onto a chopping board.
4. Place the bean mix on top and form into sausage-shaped rolls, approximately 2 cm (¾ in) wide. Sprinkle the remainder of the polenta on top and cut the rolls so that you have around 24 pieces. It's better to make smaller pieces since the gnocchi swell during cooking. Score them using a fork and roll them in the polenta that remains on the plate.
5. Place the gnocchi in boiling water – 12 pieces at a time – and leave them to simmer for around 3 minutes. They are ready when they float to the surface. Take them out and put to one side.
6. Fry the mushrooms in oil over a high heat for around 5 minutes. Add the garlic, lower the heat and fry for another minute. Add the spinach and wait for it to wilt. Season with salt and pepper. Put the mushroom and spinach mixture into a bowl.
7. Meanwhile, fry the tomatoes on the cut edge in a little oil for around 2 minutes.
8. Melt the butter in a large frying pan (skillet) and fry the gnocchi for about 3 minutes until they take on a little colour. Add the mushroom and spinach mixture.
9. Plate up the gnocchi and tomatoes. Top with Parmesan.

BEAN GNOCCHI WITH MUSHROOMS AND SPINACH (OPPOSITE)

POLENTA-BREADED COURGETTE AND TOMATO SAUCE WITH CHILLI AND LEMON (PAGE 30)

29

Polenta-breaded courgette and tomato sauce with chilli and lemon

Polenta is perfect for making porridge but it is also great for breading vegetables. Since polenta is a different Italian name for finely ground grain of maize, the small grains are also gluten free. Freekeh is a kind of green wheat that is best replaced with bulgur, but feel free to try out one of the other new mixed grains now available in shops.

SERVES 4

200 g (7 oz/1 cup) freekeh, bulgur or another mixed grain

400 g (14 oz) courgettes (zucchini)

salt and freshly ground black pepper

2–3 eggs

200 g (7 oz/1⅓ cups) finely ground polenta (cornmeal)

40 g (1½ oz) Parmesan, finely grated

60 g (2 oz/½ cup) plain (all-purpose) flour

olive oil, for frying

mint leaves and yoghurt, to serve

TOMATO SAUCE WITH CHILLI AND LEMON

1 yellow onion, diced

olive oil, for frying

2 garlic cloves, finely sliced

2 tablespoons tomato purée (paste)

500 g (1 lb 2 oz) tomatoes, diced

1 teaspoon dried oregano

½ teaspoon chilli flakes

1 tablespoon nutritional yeast

grated zest of 1 lemon

salt and freshly ground black pepper

1. Cook the grain following the instructions on the pack.
2. Cut the courgette into ½–1 cm (¼–½ in) thick slices. Season with salt and pepper.
3. For the sauce, fry the onion in oil in a saucepan for around 5 minutes over a medium-low heat until soft. Add the garlic to the pan and fry for another minute while stirring. Add the tomato purée, tomatoes and oregano, and simmer for around 10 minutes. Season with chilli flakes, nutritional yeast, lemon zest, salt and pepper.
4. Whisk the eggs in a deep dish. Mix the polenta and cheese in a different dish. Add the flour to a third dish. First turn the courgette slices in the flour, then the egg, and finally in the polenta/cheese mixture.
5. Fry the slices in hot oil in batches in a frying pan (skillet) for around 2 minutes per side until soft.
6. Serve the courgettes with the grains and tomato sauce. Sprinkle with mint leaves and serve with yoghurt.

TORTILLA PIZZA

Spread the leftover tomato sauce on tortilla wraps. Layer with thin slices of courgette (zucchini) or mushroom cut using a cheese slicer, and sprinkle cheese on top. Bake at 220°C (430°F/Gas 8) in the oven for approximately 8 minutes until the cheese is browned.

Creamy polenta with mushrooms and oven-roasted tomatoes

SERVES 4

400 g (14 oz) cherry vine tomatoes

olive oil

400 g (14 oz) mushrooms, e.g. oyster mushrooms, blushing wood mushrooms or chanterelles, rinsed and roughly chopped

2 garlic cloves, finely sliced

salt and freshly ground black pepper

400 g (13 oz/2⅔ cups) finely ground polenta (cornmeal)

75 g (2½ oz) butter

40 g (1½ oz) Parmesan, finely grated

80 g (3 oz) spinach

grated zest of 1 lemon

I didn't like polenta (cornmeal) much until I realised what the matter was: I was being too mean when it came to butter and cheese. Forget about the calories and you'll be rewarded with a creamy polenta with a distinct flavour of both corn and butter. Oyster mushrooms offer a great texture, but feel free to mix in other mushrooms.

1. Preheat the oven to 220°C (430°F/Gas 8). Put the tomatoes on a baking tray. Pour a little oil over them and roast for around 25 minutes until the tomatoes change colour.
2. Fry the mushrooms in a frying pan (skillet) without fat over a high heat for around 5 minutes. Add a little oil, reduce the heat and fry for another 10 minutes until the mushrooms are caramelised.
3. Mix the garlic with the mushrooms in the frying pan and fry for 1 minute. Season with salt and pepper to taste.
4. Cook the polenta by following the instructions on the packet and leave to simmer until it is creamy – for around 7 minutes. Stir occasionally. Stir in the butter and half of the cheese. Season with salt and pepper.
5. Stir the spinach and lemon zest into the mushroom mixture just before serving.
6. Serve the polenta with the mushroom mixture, the remainder of the cheese and the tomatoes.

VEGAN

Skip the butter and cheese. Flavour the polenta with miso, serve vegan cheese on the side and add a generous helping of olive oil when serving.

Halloumi skewers and cauliflower tabbouleh with pistachios

Just take a moment to think about all the veggies you can eat if you make tabbouleh using cauliflower instead of bulgur. Everyone has their own preferences; I love raw cauliflower. If you don't, you can boil or fry grated cauliflower for around 1 minute. If you think it's childish to eat food on skewers, then the cheese tastes just as good without the stick.

220 g (8 oz) halloumi

olive oil, for frying

salt and freshly ground black pepper

200 g (7 oz) little gem (bibb) lettuce or green salad leaves

CAULIFLOWER TABBOULEH

600 g (1 lb 5 oz) cauliflower

juice of ½ lemon

4 tablespoons mild olive oil

salt and freshly ground black pepper

2 tomatoes, seeded and finely chopped

big bunch of basil or mint leaves, roughly chopped

bunch of flat-leaf parsley, roughly chopped

75 g (2½ oz/½ cup) peeled pistachios, roughly chopped

2 spring onions (scallions), shredded

TOMATO SAUCE

2 tomatoes, halved

200 g (7 oz/1 cup) crème fraîche or yoghurt

½ teaspoon sambal oelek

1 teaspoon ground cumin

salt and freshly ground black pepper

1. Remove the green leaves from the cauliflower. Blitz the rest in a food processor or grate coarsely using a grater. Mix the lemon juice and olive oil and pour over the cauliflower. Season with salt and pepper.
2. For the sauce, fry the tomatoes in oil cut edge down over a high heat in a frying pan (skillet) until they are a little black and have softened. Leave to cool a little and then tear them apart roughly. Mix with crème fraîche or yoghurt and sambal oelek. Season with cumin, salt and pepper.
3. For the tabbouleh, mix the tomatoes, herbs, pistachios and spring onions with the cauliflower.
4. Cut the halloumi into batons and put them on skewers. Ensure that the skewers aren't too long so that they fit into the frying pan. Alternatively, you can put the cheese on the skewers after frying it. Fry for around 5 minutes until they take on some colour.
5. Tear the salad leaves apart and put on a plate, add the tabbouleh and halloumi skewers on top. Serve with the tomato sauce.

VEGAN

Serve with roasted chickpeas (garbanzos) (page 144) instead of halloumi. Use dairy-free yoghurt instead of tomato sauce.

Greek roast with green lentils and oven-baked feta

Let me go on the record straight away and tell you that this dish takes more than 30 minutes to cook. But a badly needed break while the potatoes turn crispy as they roast in the oven surely makes up for my sidestep? There are a few tricks to ensure crispiness. Use lots of oil and a hot oven. Make sure you preheat the tray so that it is really hot, and give everything an occasional shake during cooking so that the potatoes are evenly roasted and moisture is released.

1. Preheat the oven to 220°C (430°F/Gas 8) and put in a roasting pan.
2. Wash and cut the potatoes into thin wedges.
3. Take the pan out of the oven and add the potatoes and onions. Season with rosemary, salt and pepper, and drizzle plenty of oil on top. Roast for 20 minutes. Give the pan a shake, then add the tomatoes and feta. Pour a little oil onto the cheese. Roast for a further 10–15 minutes.
4. In the meantime, cook the lentils in salted water until soft, for approximately 20 minutes.
5. Mix the ingredients for the dressing. Season with salt and pepper to taste.
6. Drain the lentils and mix them with the dressing while they are still warm.
7. Pour the lentils over the potatoes and tomatoes, and sprinkle with basil leaves.

SERVES 4

1 kg (2 lb 3 oz) potatoes

2 red onions, sliced

2 teaspoons dried rosemary or 3 sprigs of rosemary

salt and freshly ground black pepper

400 g (14 oz) cherry vine tomatoes

200 g (7 oz) feta

200 g (7 fl oz/1 cup) uncooked green lentils

olive oil

basil leaves, to garnish

DRESSING

100 ml (3½ fl oz/½ cup) olive oil

2 tablespoons red wine vinegar

2 tablespoons liquid honey

2 teaspoons Dijon mustard

salt and freshly ground black pepper

SPANISH OMELETTE WITH SPINACH

Cut the leftover potatoes into smaller pieces. (It doesn't matter if a few lentils and pieces of feta are in the mix.) Peel and cut an onion into thin slices. Fry the onion in plenty of oil in a frying pan (skillet) until soft. Add the potatoes and ensure they are warmed through. Add the spinach and whisked egg. Season with salt and pepper, and fry on a low heat until the egg is just set.

SERVES 4

500 g (1 lb 2 oz) falafel
(page 175)

4 pitta breads or liba breads

sriracha or spicy tomato salsa

TAHINI DRESSING

100 ml (3½ fl oz/½ cup) tahini

1 tablespoon freshly
squeezed lemon juice

75 ml (2½ fl oz/⅓ cup) water

salt and chilli flakes

SALAD

200 g (7 oz) red cabbage

big bunch of coriander
(cilantro) leaves

2 spring onions (scallions)

225 g (8 oz) mango, diced

80 g (3 oz) salad leaves

Falafel with tahini dressing, mango and red cabbage

Ready-made falafels are great to have in the freezer for fast food dinners on home turf. I prefer to serve the fried falafel with tahini dressing, but sometimes I also make a tomato salsa or serve them with a yoghurt sauce. Falafels can be bought in a range of forms – chilled, frozen or as a dry mix. It goes without saying that homemade takes a little more planning but tastes the best.

1. Mix the tahini and lemon juice, then add enough of the water to make a creamy dressing. Season with salt and chilli flakes to taste.
2. Finely shred the red cabbage, preferably using a mandolin or cheese slicer. Roughly chop the coriander, including the stalks, and shred the spring onions. Mix everything with the mango and salad leaves.
3. Fry the falafels in a frying pan (skillet) (see instructions on the pack, if applicable).
4. Warm up the bread in the oven or in a frying pan.
5. Plate up the salad and drizzle the dressing over it. Serve with falafels and bread. If you like heat in your food, season with sriracha or spicy tomato salsa.

Wrap with tomato salsa and halloumi and falafel patties

When you tire of eating falafels in ball form, you can try adding a little salt and cheese and turning them into small patties instead. Just as solid, yet different. Good accompaniments include tomato salsa, strong pepperoncino and a sauce that you may recognise from your local kebab shop. However, I hold back on the garlic while adding a little yoghurt and seasoning the sauce with lemon zest.

4 pitta breads or liba breads

salad leaves

pepperoncino or
pickled jalapeños

FALAFEL AND HALLOUMI PATTIES

2 × 400 g (14 oz) tins
chickpeas (garbanzos)

2 teaspoons ground cumin

1 teaspoon ground coriander

pinch of chilli flakes

2 tablespoons chickpea
(gram) flour or plain
(all-purpose) flour

small bunch of coriander
(cilantro) leaves

220 g (8 oz) halloumi

rapeseed (canola)
oil, for frying

GARLIC SAUCE

1 garlic clove, grated

200 g (7 oz/1 cup) yoghurt

100 g (3½ oz/⅓ cup)
mayonnaise

grated zest of 1 lemon

salt and freshly ground
black pepper

TOMATO SALSA

3 tomatoes, finely diced

100 g (3½ oz) spring
onions (scallions)

small bunch of coriander
(cilantro) leaves

juice of ½ lemon

salt

1. To make the patties, drain the chickpeas and mix them with the spices and flour in a food processor. Chop the coriander, including the stalks. Tear the halloumi into rough pieces and mix them in. Add more flour if the batter is too runny. Shape into small patties.
2. To make the sauce, mix the garlic with the yoghurt, mayonnaise and lemon zest. Season with salt and pepper to taste.
3. To make the salsa, finely dice the tomatoes, shred the spring onions and chop the coriander. Mix with the lemon juice and season with salt.
4. Fry the patties in oil in a frying pan (skillet) for around 3 minutes per side.
5. Fill the breads with patties, tomato salsa and salad. Top with garlic sauce and pepperoncino or pickled jalapeños.

MEDITERRANEAN MAGIC

SERVES 4

2 large sweet potatoes

rapeseed (canola)
oil or olive oil

salt

4 tablespoons roughly
chopped smoked almonds
(page 176), to serve

coriander (cilantro)
leaves, to serve

pitta breads or liba
breads, to serve

WARM HUMMUS

400 g (14 oz) tin
chickpeas (garbanzos)

2 garlic cloves

4 tablespoons tahini

juice of ½ lemon

1 teaspoon ground cumin

salt

RED CABBAGE SALAD

250 g (9 oz) red cabbage

200 g (7 oz) pomegranate
seeds, preferably frozen

1 tablespoon freshly
squeezed lemon juice

1 tablespoon maple syrup

2 tablespoons olive oil

Sweet potato wedges
with warm hummus

If you've never tried warm hummus, it's time you did. By warming up the pulses, the hummus gains a perfectly rounded, strong garlic flavour. Make a double batch while you're at it in the kitchen. It keeps for up to a week in the fridge and is good in mezze, in sandwiches and in salads. If you don't have a microwave, then you can warm up the chickpeas in a saucepan on the hob. It's fine to use frozen pomegranate seeds – a gift to all stressed chefs.

1. Preheat the oven to 220°C (430°F/Gas 8).
2. Rinse and chop the sweet potatoes into thin wedges (you don't need to peel them first) and place on a baking tray lined with baking paper. Coat generously in oil and season with salt. Roast for around 20 minutes until the wedges are soft and have taken on colour. Stir once in the meantime. You can still put the potatoes in the oven even if the oven isn't up to temperature. You may need to increase the roasting time.
3. Pour the chickpeas and water into a microwave-safe bowl. Add the garlic cloves. Microwave over a high heat for around 4 minutes. Pour everything into a food processor and blend. Add the tahini, lemon juice and cumin, and mix until it is a smooth hummus. Dilute with water if necessary to ensure the right consistency, and season with salt.
4. Finely slice the red cabbage, preferably with a mandolin or cheese slicer. Mix in the pomegranate seeds.
5. Mix the lemon juice, maple syrup and oil into a dressing and pour over the cabbage.
6. Spread the hummus on the plates, add the sweet potatoes and red cabbage salad. Top with almonds and fresh coriander. Serve with pitta bread or liba bread.

Moroccan carrots with saffron bulgur and whisked 'tofotta'

Beautiful aromas spread throughout the kitchen when you fry the spices for this rich dish. Don't be put off by the long list of ingredients, which mostly consists of spices and nothing that needs chopping. Almond butter rounds off the flavours and provides a hint of toasted nuts. You can buy it from supermarkets but the dish also works fine without it. Silken tofu is good for whisking into a soft cream, not unlike Italian ricotta – hence the pun. If you're not a vegan, you can use cheese in the same way or use a dollop of yoghurt.

SERVES 4

500 g (1 lb 2 oz) carrots

5 garlic cloves, peeled

1 teaspoon ground cinnamon

1 teaspoon ground ginger

1 teaspoon paprika

2 teaspoons cumin seeds

2 teaspoons ground coriander

olive oil

400 g (14 oz) tin chopped tomatoes

250 ml (8½ fl oz/1 cup) water

400 g (14 oz) tin chickpeas (garbanzos)

2 tablespoons almond butter

agave syrup

salt and freshly ground black pepper

coriander (cilantro) and flat-leaf parsley leaves, to garnish

SAFFRON BULGUR

200 g (7 oz/1 cup) bulgur

a pinch of saffron

TOFOTTA

300 g (10½ oz) silken tofu

zest and juice of ½ lemon

salt

1. Bring a pan of salted water to the boil, or fill from the kettle.

2. Peel the carrots and cut into thin batons, approximately 5 cm (2 in) long. Cook the carrots and garlic in the boiling water for around 7 minutes until the carrots have softened somewhat but still have a hard core. Drain and leave to cool.

3. Cook the bulgur with saffron by following the instructions on the pack.

4. Toast the spices in a large saucepan or frying pan (skillet) for around 2 minutes, stirring, until they begin to give off an aroma. Add a little oil, the carrots and garlic and fry for 2 minutes while stirring. Add the tomatoes and water.

5. Drain the chickpeas, add them to the saucepan and leave to simmer for around 10 minutes with the lid on. Season with almond butter, agave syrup, salt and pepper.

6. Put the tofu in a bowl with lemon juice and lemon zest and whisk into a cream using an electric whisk. Scrape the tofu off the edges of the bowl a few times. Season with salt.

7. Serve the carrots with saffron bulgur and tofotta, and garnish with herbs.

2

POT LUCK CLUB

Heart-warming soups and delicious casseroles

If people around the world got to vote on what they would make for dinner tomorrow, the majority would probably say soup or casserole. You might wonder why. Perhaps because they offer the best value for money when it comes to flavour and nutrition. They are best served with bread, cheese or a filling salad or side dish.

Tomato soup with miso

This soup is best when made using tinned plum tomatoes – preferably San Marzano tomatoes. But use whatever you have – chopped tomatoes of unknown origin are fine. The miso provides flavour, depth and saltiness.

1. Fry the onion in oil in a saucepan over a medium-low heat for 5 minutes until soft. Add the garlic and chilli flakes. Raise the heat and fry for around 1 minute while stirring.
2. Mix in the tomatoes, stock, oregano and water. Cover with a lid and leave to simmer over a medium heat for approximately 15 minutes.
3. Pour the cream into the soup and blend until smooth. Bring to the boil again and stir in the miso. Season with salt and pepper to taste.
4. Garnish the soup with herbs and drizzle a little olive oil on top.
5. Serve the soup with toasties with vegan cheese and artichoke with cannellini beans (page 161).

SERVES 4

1 yellow onion, finely chopped

3 garlic cloves, finely chopped

½ teaspoon chilli flakes

2 × 400 g (14 oz) tins plum tomatoes

1 tablespoon concentrated vegetable stock

1 teaspoon dried oregano

400 ml (13 fl oz/1⅔ cups) water

100 ml (3½ fl oz/½ cup) dairy-free cream

2 tablespoons white miso

salt and freshly ground black pepper

herbs, e.g. thyme and basil leaves, to garnish

olive oil, for frying and to serve

Sweetcorn soup with root vegetable crisps

1 yellow onion,
finely chopped

olive oil, for frying
and to serve

2 garlic cloves,
finely chopped

2 teaspoons
ground cumin

½ teaspoon turmeric

500 g (1 lb 2 oz)
sweetcorn, frozen
or tinned

400 g (14 oz) tin cannellini
beans, drained

1 tablespoon
concentrated
vegetable stock

700 ml (23 fl oz/
2¾ cups) water

2 teaspoons freshly
squeezed lime juice

salt and chilli flakes

root vegetable
crisps, to serve

shredded spring onions
(scallions) or coriander
(cilantro), to serve

This soup is perfect for when you are too tired to go shopping and you have the good fortune to find a bag of crisps and some jars in the larder. The best-looking crisps are root vegetable crisps, but potato chips and tortilla chips are also fine. If you want an even more rounded flavour, mix 100 ml (3½ fl oz/ ½ cup) of a cream of your choice into the soup.

1. Fry the onion in oil for around 5 minutes over a medium-low heat. Add the garlic, cumin and turmeric and fry for a few minutes while stirring.
2. Mix in the sweetcorn, beans, stock and water. Cover with a lid and leave soup to simmer over a medium heat for approximately 15 minutes.
3. Blend the soup and strain it. Pour it back into saucepan and bring to the boil. Season with lime juice, salt and chilli pepper.
4. Top the soup with root vegetable crisps and spring onions or coriander. Why not drizzle a little olive oil on top, too?

SWEETCORN
SOUP WITH ROOT
VEGETABLE CRISPS
(PAGE 47)

CAULIFLOWER SOUP WITH
CURRY-FRIED APPLE AND
SEEDS (OPPOSITE)

Cauliflower soup with curry-fried apple and seeds

I don't know whether you're a genius or evil when you 'hide' protein-rich butter (lima) beans in soups. Probably the former, as the beans don't have a strong flavour but provide both nutrition and creaminess. I love it when the flavour of cauliflower is fairly pure, which is why I make my soup without vegetable stock, but you can do as you wish.

SERVES 4

1 yellow onion, diced

2 garlic cloves, crushed

olive oil, for frying
and to serve

800 g (1 lb 12 oz) cauliflower

200 g (7 oz) cooked
butter (lima) beans

500 ml (17 fl oz/2 cups) cashew
or almond milk, unsweetened

300 ml (10 fl oz/1¼ cups) water

1 tablespoon freshly
squeezed lemon juice

salt

CURRY-FRIED APPLE

1 apple, peeled,
cored and diced

olive oil, for frying

2 teaspoons curry powder

100 g (3½ oz/¾ cup)
pumpkin seeds

salt and freshly ground
black pepper

1. Fry the onion and garlic together in oil in a large saucepan for around 5 minutes until soft over a medium-low heat.
2. Remove the green leaves from the cauliflower, cut them into smaller pieces and save them. Cut the rest of the cauliflower into small pieces.
3. Mix the cauliflower, beans and nut milk into the saucepan. Add water to cover the contents, put the lid on and cook for around 15 minutes until the cauliflower is completely soft.
4. To cook the apple, put the apple and cauliflower leaves that were saved earlier into a frying pan (skillet) with a little oil, sprinkle the curry powder over it and fry until soft. Add the pumpkin seeds and ensure everything is warmed through. Season with salt and pepper.
5. Drain a little of the milk from the saucepan into a bowl. Blend the soup until it is smooth. Pour the milk back in and dilute with milk and/or water to your preferred consistency. Season with lemon juice and salt.
6. Top the soup with the fried apple and a drizzle of olive oil.

Green Thai soup with coconut cream and fried onions

SERVES 4

1 yellow onion, diced

rapeseed (canola) oil, for frying

2 garlic cloves, finely chopped

1 teaspoon green curry paste

300 g (10½ oz) frozen green peas, defrosted

500 g (1 lb 2 oz) frozen broccoli florets, defrosted

2 tablespoons concentrated vegetable stock

600 ml (20 fl oz/2½ cups) water

400 g (14 oz) tin coconut cream

1 lime

2 tablespoons white miso

Thai basil and coriander (cilantro) leaves, and crispy onions, to garnish

Sometimes I come across some vegetables at the very back of the freezer suffering from freezer burn. That's when I make this soup, and feel really good about myself and life. If you find any spinach, you can also use that. Do double check the list of ingredients in the curry paste to make sure that no dried prawns (shrimps) have crept in. The Thais do love the taste of fermented fish, so it's easily done.

1. Fry the onion in oil in a saucepan over a medium heat for approximately 5 minutes, stirring until soft. Add the garlic and curry paste. The quantity of curry paste depends on how strong it is and how hot you want the soup to be, but I recommend about a teaspoon. Raise the heat and fry for another 2 minutes while stirring.

2. Put approximately 100 g (3½ oz) peas aside for serving. Mix the rest of the peas, the broccoli, stock and water into the saucepan.

3. Whisk the tin of coconut cream and add three quarters of it to the pan. Leave the soup to simmer without a lid over a medium heat for 10–15 minutes until the vegetables have fully softened.

4. Blend the soup in a food processor until it is smooth, then pour it back into the saucepan (or use a hand-held blender). Dilute with water if you think it's too thick.

5. Season the soup with the juice of half the lime and the miso.

6. Pour the soup into bowls, drizzle the rest of the coconut cream on top and sprinkle with the extra peas, herbs and crispy onions. Cut the rest of the lime into wedges and serve alongside.

1 yellow onion, diced

2 garlic cloves, crushed

olive oil, for frying
and to serve

1 teaspoon ground cumin

1 teaspoon ground coriander

50 g (2 oz) ginger

700 g (1 lb 9 oz) carrots,
peeled and coarsely grated

2 tablespoons concentrated
vegetable stock

1 litre (34 fl oz/4 cups) water

salt

200 g (7 oz/1 cup) dairy-
free yoghurt, to serve

ORANGE-MARINATED LENTILS

100 g (3½ oz/½ cup)
dried red lentils

big bunch of flat-leaf
parsley or coriander
(cilantro) leaves, chopped

1 spring onion (scallion),
finely shredded

juice of ½ orange

½ teaspoon harissa
or chilli flakes

1 teaspoon ground cumin

2 tablespoons olive oil

salt

Carrot soup with orange-marinated lentils

Carrot is a great fit with ginger, cumin and sour yoghurt – the perfect ingredients for a tasty soup. Are you a carrot enthusiast? Replace the water with carrot juice for a more intense carrot flavour. Harissa is a strong North African spice paste made with ingredients that include chilli, garlic, cumin, caraway and coriander seeds. If you eat dairy products, you can use high-fat yoghurt instead of the vegan alternative.

1. Fry the onion and garlic in a little oil in a saucepan until soft for around 5 minutes over a medium-low heat while stirring. Raise the heat, add the spices and fry for 2 minutes while stirring.
2. Peel and finely grate the ginger, squeeze out the juice and save it. Discard the remains.
3. Add the carrots, ginger juice, stock and water to the pan. Simmer over a medium heat for around 15 minutes under a lid until the carrots are soft.
4. In the meantime, boil the lentils in salted water according to the instructions on page 171.
5. Combine the rest of the ingredients for the orange marinade and pour over the lentils while they are still warm. Season with salt.
6. Blend the soup until smooth and season again with salt, to taste. Warm it up again and, if necessary, dilute with more water.
7. Top the soup with the lentil mixture and a dollop of yoghurt. Drizzle lightly with olive oil.

Spicy miso ramen with eggs and soybeans

Cooking the popular Japanese ramen soup from scratch normally takes a long time. But with a little help from ingredients rich in umami, like shiitake mushrooms, miso, nutritional yeast and stock – you can make a good broth in just half an hour. If you can't find fresh shiitake mushrooms, it's fine to use a smaller quantity of dried ones, which should be soaked in water first.

SERVES 4

4 eggs, soft-boiled

150 g (5 oz) fresh shiitake mushrooms, sliced

rapeseed (canola) oil, for frying

250 g (9 oz) Chinese cabbage

2 garlic cloves, finely chopped

2 tablespoons concentrated chanterelle stock or vegetable stock

1.8 litres (62 fl oz/ 7¼ cups) water

200 g (7 oz) dried noodles or 500 g (1 lb 2 oz) fresh noodles

5 tablespoons white miso

4 tablespoons nutritional yeast

1–2 tablespoons sriracha

200 g (7 oz) soybeans, defrosted

100 g (3½ oz) sweetcorn

25 g (1 oz) butter

furikake (page 179) or roasted sesame seeds

sesame oil and sriracha, to serve

VEGAN

Skip the eggs and butter. Crumble in a little tofu for extra protein.

1. Rinse the eggs in cold water.
2. Fry the mushrooms in rapeseed oil for around 5 minutes until they take on some colour.
3. Remove four good-looking leaves from the Chinese cabbage and finely shred the remainder. Mix the garlic and cabbage with the mushrooms and fry for a further 2 minutes while stirring.
4. Add the stock and water, and leave to simmer without a lid over a medium heat for 10–15 minutes.
5. Add the noodles and cook according to instructions on the pack, or cook them in a separate saucepan.
6. Peel the eggs and halve them.
7. Season the soup with miso, nutritional yeast and sriracha. Bring the soup back to the boil to ensure it is really hot.
8. Place the reserved cabbage leaves into the soup bowls. Pour the soup in and top with eggs, spring onions, soybeans, sweetcorn, butter and furikake or sesame seeds. Drizzle a little sesame oil on top.
9. You can also serve with sriracha on the side to cater for anyone who wants a soup with more kick.

SERVES 4

300 g (10½ oz/1⅔ cups) jasmine rice

2 garlic cloves, finely chopped

700 ml (23 fl oz/2¾ cups) rapeseed (canola) oil, for frying and deep-frying

1–2 tablespoons red curry paste

200 g (7 oz/1 cup) dried red lentils

600 ml (20 fl oz/2½ cups) water

400 g (14 oz) tin coconut cream

4 large sheets of rice paper

zest and juice of 1 lime

80 g (3 oz) baby spinach

salt

coriander (cilantro) leaves, to garnish

Red lentil curry with rice paper crisps

Paper crisps may sound rather dry, but it truly is an exciting event in the kitchen when the rice paper puffs up in the hot oil. If you aren't comfortable deep-frying or think it's unhealthy, just skip for a less eventful evening. The curry paste varies in strength, so start with a tablespoon, taste it, and add more if you want a hotter dish.

1. Cook the rice following the instructions on the pack.
2. Fry the garlic in oil in a saucepan for around 2 minutes over a medium heat until soft. Add the curry paste, raise the heat and fry for another 1 minute while stirring.
3. Add the lentils and water. Whisk the coconut cream so that it is mixed, then pour three-quarters into the saucepan. Simmer over a medium heat for around 15 minutes until the lentils are soft.
4. Deep-fry one rice paper sheet at a time in hot oil in a large saucepan for around 1 minute. Place them on kitchen paper when they are done.
5. Mix the spinach into the lentil curry and ensure it warms through. Season with salt and approximately 1 tablespoon lime juice.
6. If you have time, you can whisk the lime zest into the coconut cream you saved, using an electric whisk. Otherwise, you can simply mix them together.
7. Top the curry with the lime-coconut cream and coriander leaves. Serve with the paper crisps and rice.

FRIED RICE BALLS WITH CHEESE AND CABBAGE

Mix any leftover rice with mature grated cheese and whisked eggs to form a creamy batter that holds together. Form into small circles and put a piece of butter-fried, fennel-spiced black kale or spinach in the middle. Press together to form balls, then roll them in flour, in the whisked egg and finally in panko breadcrumbs mixed with sesame seeds. Fry the balls in hot oil until crispy.

1 yellow onion, finely chopped

3 garlic cloves, finely chopped

rapeseed (canola)
oil, for frying

50 g (2 oz) ginger, peeled
and finely grated

1 teaspoon ground coriander

2 teaspoons garam masala

1 tablespoon tomato
purée (paste)

400 g (14 oz) tin
chopped tomatoes

400 g (14 oz) tin chickpeas
(garbanzos), drained

300 ml (10 fl oz/1¼ cups) water

1 tablespoon agave syrup

salt

4 poppadoms, to serve

chopped coriander
(cilantro) leaves and
mango chutney, to serve

YELLOW CAULIFLOWER RICE

600 g (1 lb 5 oz) cauliflower

½ teaspoon turmeric

rapeseed (canola)
oil, for frying

Chana masala with yellow cauliflower rice

Chana means 'chickpeas' and masala means 'spices', and that is exactly what this is: spicy chickpeas in a tomato sauce. Serve alongside yellow cauliflower rice and poppadoms, which are easy to make in the microwave. If you eat dairy products, there are plenty of great options. For example, you can add a knob of butter to the cauliflower rice and round off the dish with yoghurt.

1. Fry the onion and garlic in oil over a medium-low heat in a frying pan (skillet) for approximately 5 minutes until soft. Squeeze the juice from the ginger and discard the remains. Add the spices and tomato purée, raise the heat and fry for another 2 minutes while stirring. Add the ginger juice, tinned tomatoes, drained chickpeas and water, and simmer for approximately 10 minutes.

2. In the meantime, make the cauliflower rice. Remove the green outer leaves from the cauliflower, but save them. Chop the cauliflower into rough pieces or make a fine rice using a food processor. Put the rice on a tea towel and squeeze to remove any moisture. Fry with the turmeric in a frying pan with a little oil for around 7 minutes. Stir occasionally.

3. Mix the cauliflower leaves into the tomato sauce and boil for a further 5 minutes. Season with agave syrup and salt to taste.

4. Put poppadoms into the microwave one at a time and cook on full power. Do this in 15-second bursts, as they burn easily. Alternatively, you can fry them in hot oil for a few seconds.

5. Sprinkle the coriander leaves over the dish and serve with cauliflower rice, poppadoms and mango chutney.

INDIAN TOMATO CASSEROLE WITH EGGS

Fry finely diced yellow onions until soft in oil in a frying pan (skillet). Add some ground cumin and cumin seeds and fry a little more. Add the leftover curry and cauliflower rice, as well as chopped tomatoes and leave to simmer. Crack one or more eggs into the pan, put the lid on and simmer until the egg whites have set, 5–10 minutes. Serve with naan bread and paneer or fried halloumi.

Palak paneer

300 g (10½ oz/1½ cups) rice,
e.g. basmati or brown rice

1 yellow onion, diced

1–2 green chillies,
seeded and sliced

2 garlic cloves, finely chopped

1 tablespoon garam masala

2 teaspoons ground cumin

3 tomatoes, diced or 400 g
(14 oz) tin chopped tomatoes

50 g (2 oz) ginger

200 ml (7 fl oz/¾ cup) cream

100 ml (3½ fl oz/½ cup) water

300 g (10½ oz) baby spinach

salt

400 g (14 oz) paneer (page 176)

oil, for frying

lime wedges, coriander
(cilantro) leaves and
coconut chips, for serving

VEGAN

Use dairy-free cream and
firm tofu instead of paneer.
You can spice the tofu with
a little garam masala.

This is one my very favourite Indian vegetarian dishes – a creamy curry with spinach and cheese. Paneer is available to buy in well-stocked Asian stores (often frozen) or you can make it at home by following the recipe on page 175. Halloumi or tofu work well as alternatives – the taste isn't the same, but it is delicious, which is good enough for me. I've left the spinach whole here, but if you want to serve it like they do in Indian restaurants, you should blend the greens before adding the cheese. Is your tummy already rumbling? You could also mix some cooked green lentils into the dish.

1. Cook the rice following the instructions on the pack.
2. Fry the onion in a little oil in a large saucepan for around 5 minutes over a medium-low heat until soft.
3. Fry the chilli, garlic, garam masala and cumin together with the onion for a minute or so while stirring. Add the tomatoes and fry for another 5 minutes until the tomatoes have softened.
4. Peel and grate the ginger and keep the juice. Discard the remains. Mix in the cream, water and ginger juice and simmer for a few minutes. Mix in the spinach and wait for it to wilt. Season with salt. Blend the sauce if you like.
5. Cube the cheese and fry it in oil in a frying pan (skillet). Place on top of the spinach base.
6. Serve with rice, lime wedges, coriander and coconut chips.

4 garlic cloves

1 yellow onion, diced

olive oil or butter, for frying

3 firm potatoes

500 g (1 lb 2 oz) sweet potato

200 g (7 oz) celeriac (celery
roots), peeled and diced

a pinch of saffron

2 teaspoons curry powder

2 × 400 g (14 oz) tins
cherry tomatoes

Parmesan rind

600 ml (20 fl oz/2½ cups) water

400 g (14 oz) tin butter
(lima) beans

4 slices of multigrain bread

100 g (3½ oz) chopped
herbs, e.g. flat-leaf parsley,
basil leaves or dill

miso, salt, honey
and chilli flakes

PARMESAN CREAM

100 g (3½ oz/⅓ cup)
mayonnaise

4 tablespoons finely
grated Parmesan

VEGAN

Replace the Parmesan
cream with a mixture
of egg-free mayonnaise
(page 174) and vegan cheese.
Skip the cheese rind.

Vegetable stew with saffron, curry and Parmesan cream

There are many good things that can be said about sweet potatoes: they're good-looking, easy to peel and quick to cook. Most importantly, they're delicious – especially when partnered with acidic tomatoes and lots of spices. This stew contains an unusual ingredient – cheese rind – which provides the umami flavour. The miso also provides umami, but can be skipped.

1. Peel the garlic, save one clove and finely chop the remainder. Fry the onion in oil in a saucepan over a medium-low heat for around 5 minutes until soft.
2. In the meantime, peel the potatoes and sweet potato and cut them into 1 cm (½ in) cubes.
3. Add the celeriac and chopped garlic to the saucepan and raise the heat. Leave to fry for another few minutes while stirring.
4. Add the potatoes, spices, tomatoes, cheese rind and water and boil with the lid on for 10 minutes. Rinse the beans, add them, and leave to simmer for another 5–10 minutes until the potatoes are tender.
5. Meanwhile, split the remaining garlic clove in the middle and rub the cut edges on the bread. Sprinkle the herbs on top. Fry the bread in oil or butter in a frying pan (skillet).
6. Mix the mayonnaise and Parmesan.
7. Remove the cheese rind from the stew and season with miso, salt, honey and chilli flakes.
8. Serve the stew with bread and Parmesan cream.

TOMATO SOUP WITH GRILLED PEPPERS

Mix any leftover soup and bread – ideally the garlic-fried bread – with grilled peppers and tinned plum tomatoes in a food processor. Season with salt, pepper, vinegar and Tabasco sauce. Add water to achieve the consistency of a thick soup. Heat the soup or serve it cold with an ice cube as a gazpacho.

SERVES 4

1 large yellow onion, diced

oil, for frying

4 large potatoes

700 g (1 lb 9 oz) cauliflower

1 teaspoon ground cumin

2 teaspoons curry powder

1½ teaspoons cardamom
seeds, crushed

2 tablespoons concentrated
vegetable stock

700 ml (23 fl oz/2¾ cups) water

200 ml (7 fl oz/¾ cup)
dairy-free cream

40 g (1½ oz) ginger

300 g (10½ oz/2 cups)
green peas

salt and lime juice

big bunch of coriander
(cilantro) leaves, to serve

bread, e.g. naan bread,
or rice, to serve

NUT AND COCONUT MIX

50 g (2 oz/⅓ cup) roasted
salted cashews,
roughly chopped

zest of 1 lime

100 g (3½ oz/2 cups)
toasted coconut chips

Mild Indian cauliflower korma with curry and green peas

This is a mild curry with warm spices like cumin and cardamom. The ginger provides a little heat, and if you want more of that you can add one or two finely chopped green chillies. The curry turns out differently depending on what kind of potatoes you use. A floury type thickens the dish, while a firm potato keeps its shape and makes the dish thinner.

1. Fry the onion in plenty of oil in a saucepan for around 5 minutes over a low heat until soft.
2. Peel and dice the potatoes into 1 cm (½ in) cubes. Chop the cauliflower into smaller pieces. Save the cauliflower leaves.
3. Raise the heat and add all the spices to the saucepan with the onion. Fry for another minute or so while stirring. Add the potatoes and stir while mixing in the cauliflower, stock, water and cream. Leave to simmer under a lid for approximately 15 minutes until the potatoes are tender.
4. In the meantime, peel and grate the ginger. Squeeze the juice out and stir into the pan.
5. Mix the roasted nuts with the lime zest and coconut chips.
6. Add the cauliflower leaves and peas to the curry and let them warm through. Add more water if it boils off. Season with salt and lime juice to taste.
7. Top with the nut and coconut mixture. Garnish with coriander and serve with bread or rice.

POTATO SOUP WITH COCONUT MILK

Fry a finely chopped yellow onion in a saucepan with oil. Add some grated ginger and a little finely chopped chilli, and fry for a little longer. Add the leftover soup, concentrated vegetable stock, coconut cream and water. Simmer and then blend the soup until it is smooth. Season with some more spices and salt.

VEGAN

Skip the eggs and use tofu instead. Replace the dairy products with plant-based alternatives.

EGG AND TOMATO

Shakshuka is a stew from the Middle East made with eggs and tomatoes. Similar dishes are served in many other places around the world, such as Mexico's huevos rancheros and Turkey's menemen. There isn't a British equivalent, but you can always borrow a few known flavours and make your own version. Eggs and tomatoes are a great match.

SERVES 4

1 yellow onion, diced

olive oil, for frying and to garnish

2 garlic cloves, finely chopped

1 teaspoon ground coriander

1 teaspoon ground cumin

2 × 400 g (14 oz) tins chopped tomatoes

400 g (14 oz) tin kidney beans

salt and freshly ground black pepper

4–8 eggs, depending on the size of your frying pan (skillet)

4 pitta breads or cooked bulgur

herbs, to garnish

TAHINI DRESSING

5 tablespoons tahini

1 tablespoon freshly squeezed lemon juice

2 pinches of paprika

75 ml (2½ fl oz/⅓ cup) water

salt and freshly ground black pepper

Shakshuka with kidney beans and tahini

1. Fry the onion in oil for around 5 minutes in a large frying pan (skillet) over a medium-low heat until soft. Add the garlic and spices, raise the heat and fry for another few minutes while stirring.
2. Add the tinned tomatoes and simmer for around 10 minutes.
3. Drain the beans and stir them in. Season with salt and pepper to taste. Ensure the mixture is warmed through.
4. Form a cavity in the middle of the sauce and crack an egg into it. Repeat with the rest of the eggs. Put a lid on the pan and simmer for 5–10 minutes until the egg whites have set but the yolks remain runny.
5. In the meantime, mix the ingredients for the tahini dressing. Add water to achieve the desired consistency. Season with salt and pepper.
6. Warm up the bread either in a frying pan or in the oven.
7. Top the tomato stew with herbs, drizzle some tahini dressing and olive oil on top. Serve with bread or bulgur.

Menemen with feta and dill

SERVES 4

1 white onion, finely chopped

2 garlic cloves, finely chopped

olive oil, for frying

1 green pepper, seeded and finely chopped

2 × 400 g (14 oz) tins cherry tomatoes

1 teaspoon chilli flakes

8 eggs

100 g (3½ oz) feta

salt and freshly ground black pepper

4 slices of light sourdough bread

dill, to garnish

1. Fry the onion and garlic together in a little oil in a large frying pan (skillet) for around 5 minutes over a medium-low heat until soft.
2. Add the pepper and let it fry for another few minutes until it softens. Add the tomatoes and chilli flakes, and simmer for around 5–10 minutes.
3. Crack the eggs into a bowl, whisk them and crumble three-quarters of the feta into the mixture. Pour the egg mixture into the tomato mixture and mix until it solidifies like scrambled eggs. Season with salt and pepper.
4. Fry the bread in a frying pan with a little oil until crispy.
5. Top the stew with dill and the rest of the feta. Serve with the bread and mashed beans with dill (page 156).

Korean tomato stew with kimchi and tofu

SERVES 4

1 yellow onion, diced

rapeseed (canola) oil and sesame oil

2 garlic cloves, finely chopped

2 tablespoons tomato purée (paste)

2 × 400 g (14 oz) tins chopped tomatoes

200 g (7 oz) kimchi

2 tablespoons white miso

honey

salt

4–8 eggs, depending on the size of your frying pan (skillet)

75 g (2½ oz) spring onions (scallions)

200 g (7 oz) silken tofu

multigrain bread or tortilla wraps, rice or potato rösti, to serve

1. Fry the onion in rapeseed oil in a large saucepan over a medium-low heat for around 5 minutes until soft. Add the garlic and tomato purée. Raise the heat and fry for another minute while stirring.
2. Add the tinned tomatoes and simmer for around 10 minutes.
3. Add the kimchi and miso. Season with honey and salt to taste.
4. Form a cavity in the middle of the sauce and crack an egg into it. Repeat with the rest of the eggs. Put a lid on the pan and simmer for 5–10 minutes until the egg whites have set but the yolks remain runny.
5. Shred the spring onions.
6. Crumble the tofu over the tomato stew and top with spring onions and a few drops of sesame oil.
7. Serve with bread, rice or potato rösti (coarsely grated potato fried in butter into small circles).

MENEMEN
WITH FETA
AND DILL
(PAGE 67)

SHAKSHUKA WITH
KIDNEY BEANS AND
TAHINI (PAGE 66)

Huevos rancheros with black beans, jalapeños and sour cream

SERVES 4

1 yellow onion, diced

rapeseed (canola) oil, for frying

2 garlic cloves, finely chopped

1 teaspoon ground coriander

1 teaspoon ground cumin

1 teaspoon paprika

2 × 400 g (14 oz) tins chopped tomatoes

400 g (14 oz) tin black beans

salt and freshly ground black pepper

4–8 eggs, depending on the size of your frying pan (skillet)

4–8 tortilla wraps

pickled jalapeños, sour cream, coriander (cilantro) leaves and feta, to garnish

1. Fry the onion in a little oil in a large frying pan (skillet) for around 5 minutes over a medium-low heat until soft. Add the garlic and spices, raise the heat and fry for another minute or so while stirring.
2. Add the tinned tomatoes and simmer for around 10 minutes.
3. Drain the beans and stir them in. Season with salt and pepper to taste. Ensure the mixture is warmed through.
4. Form a cavity in the middle of the sauce and crack an egg into it. Repeat with the rest of the eggs. Put a lid on the pan and simmer for 5–10 minutes until the egg whites have set but the yolks remain runny.
5. Warm up the wraps either in a dry frying pan or in the oven.
6. Top the tomato stew with sliced jalapeños, sour cream, coriander and crumbled feta. Serve with the bread.

HUEVOS RANCHEROS
WITH BLACK BEANS,
JALAPEÑOS AND SOUR
CREAM (ABOVE)

KOREAN TOMATO
STEW WITH KIMCHI
AND TOFU (PAGE 67)

3
CROWD PLEASERS

*Pizza, burgers,
pancakes and tacos*

If you're feeding someone who doesn't eat
vegetarian very often, it's a good idea to cook
them something they already eat without
realising it's vegetarian. Pancakes are a good
example. Other crowd pleasers include tasty
pizzas, delicious burgers and spicy Mexican
dishes. That's the kind of food most
people like.

Bean burger with avocado cream

The Incas were a smart bunch. They would throw chillies onto the open fire to preserve them, but also because of the great smoky flavour it gave them. You don't need to do this. Instead, you can buy chipotles – smoked jalapeños – as a paste (often found in the Tex-Mex section of the supermarket), as a finely ground spice or as a sauce (an adobo). You can skip both the chipotle and the nutritional yeast. Add potato wedges to turn this burgers into real cowboy food – in other words, they're filling! A good tip is to make a double batch of burgers and put some in the freezer unfried.

SERVES 4

1 egg

100 g (3½ oz/1⅔ cups) panko breadcrumbs

100–200 g (3½–7 oz/ 1–2 cups) almond flour

1–2 teaspoons chipotle paste

1 teaspoon ground cumin

2 tablespoons nutritional yeast

400 g (14 oz) tin black beans, drained

small bunch of coriander (cilantro) leaves

salt

sesame seeds or panko breadcrumbs, for coating

rapeseed (canola) oil, for frying

AVOCADO CREAM

2 avocados

1 garlic clove, finely chopped

1 teaspoon freshly squeezed lime juice

small bunch of coriander (cilantro) leaves

salt and chilli flakes

TO SERVE

4 slices cheese, e.g. Cheddar

4 hamburger buns

salad leaves

tomato slices

Sweet Potato Wedges (page 41) or frozen potato wedges

1. Whisk the egg in a bowl and mix with the panko breadcrumbs, almond flour, chipotle, cumin and nutritional yeast. Add the beans and gently crush them using a wooden spoon until some are mashed. Stir to form a firm mixture. Chop the coriander, including the stalks, and add to the mix. Season with salt.

2. Shape the mixture into four round burgers. Coat them in sesame seeds or panko breadcrumbs, or a mixture of both.

3. For the avocado cream, remove the stone from the avocado and mix the flesh with the garlic and lime juice to form a cream. Chop the coriander, including the stalks, add to the avocado and season with salt and chilli.

4. Fry the patties in oil for around 3 minutes per side until they are golden.

5. Place the slices of cheese on the burgers.

6. Spread the avocado cream on the bottom half of the bread. Add the salad, tomatoes and bean burgers to the top. Serve with potato wedges.

QUESADILLA WITH BEANS

Spread spicy tomato salsa on tortilla wraps. Sprinkle some chunks of bean burger and grated cheese on top – preferably both mature cheese and mozzarella. Fold together and fry the quesadilla in a frying pan (skillet) with some oil until golden.

CROWD PLEASERS

Portobello burgers with truffle bean cream

Large chestnut mushrooms are sometimes sold under the lovely name 'Portobello'. If you can't find any, normal mushrooms will do fine. The taste is the same, but you will need to lay the table with knives and forks since the mushrooms are small and can easily fall out of the buns. Don't like kale? Use ordinary green salad instead, or serve with a side such as hari fries (page 147).

(page 147)

SERVES 4

4 large **Portobello** mushrooms, trimmed

1 tablespoon olive oil, plus extra for frying

3 red onions, sliced

75 g (2½ oz) kale

4 slices cheese, e.g. gruyère or **Cheddar**

2 tablespoons balsamic vinegar

1 tablespoon liquid honey

4 hamburger buns, to serve

tomato slices, to serve

TRUFFLE BEAN CREAM

400 g (14 oz) tin cannellini beans

3 tablespoons crème fraîche

zest and juice of 1 lemon

1½ tablespoon nutritional yeast

dash of truffle oil

VEGAN

Skip the crème fraîche. Use vegan cheese and swap the honey for agave syrup.

1. Fry the whole mushrooms in oil in a frying pan (skillet) over a medium heat for around 5 minutes until soft.
2. Add the onions and fry for another 10 minutes.
3. To make the cream, drain the beans and mash them with the crème fraîche to form a cream. Flavour the bean cream with the lemon zest, approximately 1 teaspoon lemon juice, the nutritional yeast and a few drops of truffle oil. Be careful not to make the truffle flavour too strong.
4. Shred the kale leaves into smaller pieces and put them in a bowl. Massage in the remainder of the lemon juice and 1 tablespoon olive oil.
5. Place the cheese on the mushrooms so that it melts. Remove the mushrooms from the frying pan and put to one side. Pour the balsamic vinegar and honey into the frying pan with the onions and cook for a minute or so.
6. In another frying pan, toast the buns with or without fat.
7. Put a burger in each bun and top with mushrooms, red onion, bean cream, kale and tomatoes.

Halloumi and courgette burger with lemon coleslaw

Warm cheese on bread could very well be the eighth wonder of the world. And given that potatoes fried in fat are probably the ninth, you might as well serve them together. All approaches are good, but rosemary potato wedges feel like a suitable Greek-style side dish.

SERVES 4

400 g (14 oz) courgettes (zucchini)

300 g (10½ oz) halloumi

200 g (7 oz/1¾ cups) chickpea (gram) flour or plain (all-purpose) flour

2–3 eggs, beaten

300 g (10½ oz/5 cups) panko breadcrumbs

salt

rapeseed (canola) oil, for frying

LEMON COLESLAW

200 g (7 oz/¾ cup) mayonnaise

zest and juice of ½ lemon

salt, sugar and chilli flakes

1 large carrot, peeled and coarsely grated

200 g (7 oz) white cabbage, shredded

TO SERVE

4 large slices of sourdough bread

salad leaves

tomato slices

pickled jalapeños or pepperoncino

1. Cut the courgette into 5 mm (¼ in) thick slices. Salt the slices and put on a plate.
2. To make the coleslaw, mix the mayonnaise, lemon zest and juice. Season with salt, sugar and chilli flakes to taste. Mix in the carrot and cabbage.
3. Cut the halloumi into four or eight slices. Pat the halloumi and courgette slices dry using kitchen paper. First turn them in flour, then in whisked egg, and finally in the panko breadcrumbs. Fry in oil until golden in batches or, if possible, using two frying pans (skillets).
4. Toast the bread, if desired. Add salad leaves, tomato slices, coleslaw, courgettes, halloumi and jalapeños or pepperoncino, as preferred.

600 g (1 lb 5 oz) oyster mushrooms, rinsed and roughly chopped

1 yellow onion, finely chopped

1 garlic clove, finely chopped

rapeseed (canola) oil, for frying

1 teaspoon ground cumin

½ teaspoon paprika

100 ml (3½ fl oz/½ cup) barbecue sauce, preferably with hickory flavour

1 tablespoon agave syrup

salt and freshly ground black pepper

TO SERVE

2 avocados

salad leaves

4 tablespoons salted peanuts, chopped

Lemon-marinated red onion (page 152)

tortilla wraps

coriander (cilantro) leaves

Pulled oyster mushrooms with lemon-marinated red onion

This is real comfort food that is also pretty easy to make. The quantity of syrup depends on how sweet your barbecue sauce is. Adjust the flavour so that it is balanced on the intersection between sweet, smoky and hot. Great served with oven-roasted potatoes or sweet potato wedges. Corn on the cob or mashed black beans (page 94) are also good options.

1. Fry the mushrooms in a large frying pan (skillet) without oil for approximately 5 minutes over a high heat until they have taken on colour and some of the liquid has steamed off.
2. Add the onion, garlic, a little oil and the spices and lower the heat. Fry over a medium heat for 5–10 minutes until the mushrooms and onion are soft. Add the barbecue sauce and agave syrup and allow to simmer. Season with salt and pepper.
3. Remove the stones from the avocados and chop the flesh.
4. Place the avocado, salad leaves, mushrooms, peanuts and lemon-marinated red onion on tortilla wraps. Garnish with coriander.

SERVES 4

250 g (9 oz) blanched almonds or cashews

1 yellow onion, diced

rapeseed (canola) oil, for frying

2–4 tablespoons taco seasoning (page 179)

200 ml (7 fl oz/¾ cup) water

1 iceberg lettuce

WARM SWEETCORN SALSA

200 g (7 oz) sweetcorn, frozen, tinned or fresh

1 red chilli, seeded and finely chopped

2 tomatoes, diced

75 g (2½ oz) spring onions (scallions), finely shredded

zest and juice of ½ lime

rapeseed (canola) oil, for frying

salt

ACCOMPANIMENTS

Shredded red cabbage, diced tomatoes, grated carrots, diced mango (frozen), diced pineapple (frozen), coriander leaves, chilli sauce, guacamole or sliced avocado, sour cream, grated cheese, etc.

Salad tacos with warm sweetcorn salsa

When you blend almonds or nuts just right, it looks almost like mince. I don't know whether that's a good thing, but it's a fact. If you soak the almonds or nuts before blending them, it makes them healthier and easier to break down. If you soak them for longer than four hours, they end up too soft to make mince with but are great for mixing into cream. Serve your tacos with whatever accompaniments you prefer, have time to prepare, and which suit your concept.

1. If possible, soak the nuts in hot water for a maximum of 2 hours. Drain the water.
2. Blend the nuts, ideally in a food processor, but not too finely.
3. Fry the onion in oil in a frying pan (skillet) for around 5 minutes over a medium heat until soft. Add the blended nuts, taco spice and water, and boil for approximately 10 minutes.
4. Separate the lettuce into individual leaves and place them in ice-cold water to make them crispy.
5. To make the salsa, drain any liquid from the sweetcorn and dry them using kitchen paper. Fry the sweetcorn in a little oil in a frying pan (skillet) over a high heat for around 7 minutes.
6. Mix the chilli, tomatoes and spring onions with the sweetcorn in the saucepan.
7. Season the sweetcorn salsa with the lime zest, lime juice and salt.
8. Place the mince in the salad leaves and serve with the sweetcorn salsa and accompaniments of your choice.

Taco-style corn fritters

SERVES 4

450 g (1 lb) sweetcorn, frozen or fresh from around 3 corn cobs

150 g (5 oz/1¼ cups) cornflour (cornstarch) or chickpea (gram) flour

1 teaspoon baking powder (baking soda)

½ teaspoon chilli flakes

¾ teaspoon salt

2 eggs

rapeseed (canola) oil, for frying

MILD GUACAMOLE WITH BUTTER BEANS

2 avocados

200 g (7 oz) cooked butter (lima) beans

juice of ½ lime

1 garlic clove, finely chopped

salt

water

ACCOMPANIMENTS

Tortilla wraps, shredded red cabbage, diced tomatoes, grated carrots, diced mango (frozen), diced pineapple (frozen), coriander leaves, salad, chilli sauce, sour cream, grated cheese, etc.

My youngest doesn't jump for joy for when I say I'm making vegetarian food for dinner. The exception to this is when I make corn fritters. I laugh to myself when he helps himself to the mild bean guacamole. Pick the accompaniments you like and that you think are best for a taco-fest. I usually make adult-friendly fritters by adding some finely chopped chilli, shredded spring onions (scallions) and coriander (cilantro) to half the batter.

1. Remove the stone from the avocados for the guacamole and mash or mix the flesh with the beans and lime juice. Mix in the garlic and season with salt. Add enough water to achieve your preferred consistency.
2. Dry the sweetcorn using kitchen paper.
3. Mix the flour with baking powder, chilli flakes and salt.
4. Crack the eggs and separate the yolks from the whites. Whisk the egg whites in a bowl until stiff. Gently beat the yolks in a separate bowl. Tip the sweetcorn and flour in with the yolks. Then turn in the egg whites and fold in gently.
5. Dollop small corn fritters into a frying pan (skillet) with plenty of oil. You will need to cook them in batches. Fry them for around 2 minutes per side until they are golden.
6. Serve with the guacamole and accompaniments of your choice.

SALAD TACOS WITH WARM SWEETCORN SALSA (PAGE 80)

CROWD PLEASERS

Nachos with sweetcorn, cheese, beans and tomato salsa

Nachos are often served as snacks in bars. With beans, sweetcorn and healthier chips made using tortilla wraps, they also have a place on the dinner table – preferably served with salad or rice to make for a more filling meal. If your desire for kale is unbearable, you can always add a few leaves in the final minutes before removing the nachos from the oven. Remember that the cooking time for the sweetcorn varies by type and season, so set your time by 5-minute increments.

1. Preheat the oven to 200°C (400°F/Gas 6).
2. Boil the corn cobs in a saucepan with salted water until soft. Cut them into smaller pieces.
3. Cut the tortilla wraps into triangles using a pair of scissors. Put them on a baking tray lined with baking paper and drizzle with oil. Sprinkle the sesame seeds on top. Bake the tortilla triangles in the oven for approximately 5 minutes until they have dried and are beginning to take on some colour. Move them around once during baking, as they burn easily.
4. In the meantime, drain the beans. Mash them and mix with 100 g (3½ oz) of spicy tomato salsa and the cumin.
5. Take the tortilla triangles out of the oven and cover with the mashed beans. Grate the mozzarella over the top. Bake for another 5 minutes until the cheese has melted.
6. Mix the tomatoes with the remainder of the spicy tomato salsa.
7. Pour the tomato salsa onto the chips. Remove the stone from the avocado, chop the flesh into pieces and add it, with some chopped coriander leaves to garnish. If you like, drizzle some sour cream on top.

SERVES 4

3 corn cobs, frozen or fresh

200 g (7 oz) tortilla wraps

2 tablespoons rapeseed (canola) oil

2 tablespoons sesame seeds

400 g (14 oz) tin black beans

200 g (7 oz) tomato salsa, preferably spicy

1 teaspoon ground cumin

230 g (8 oz) mozzarella

2 tomatoes, seeded and finely chopped

1 avocado

chopped coriander (cilantro) leaves and sour cream, to garnish

VEGAN

Use vegan cheese instead of mozzarella and skip the sour cream.

Sweet potato patties with halloumi and fried eggs

SERVES 4

500 g (1 lb 2 oz) broccoli
or broccolini

200 g (7 oz/1 cup) quinoa

80 g (3 oz) spinach leaves

1 garlic clove, finely sliced

4 eggs

salt and freshly ground
black pepper

SWEET POTATO PATTIES

3 eggs

5 tablespoons panko
breadcrumbs

1 tablespoon cornflour
(cornstarch) or chickpea
(gram) flour

200 g (7 oz) halloumi,
coarsely grated

300 g (10½ oz) sweet potato,
peeled and coarsely grated

salt and freshly ground
black pepper

rapeseed (canola)
oil, for frying

These are a bit like rösti or hash browns, but are so different that you can't really use either name for this dish. 'Crispy patties with runny eggs' might be closer to the truth. Or why not simply 'delicious patties'? To pull this one off in half an hour, you need to use two frying pans (skillets) at once. If that's too much, you can skip the eggs and spinach, and serve the patties with a sauce made from yoghurt, mayonnaise and chilli sauce instead.

1. Whisk the eggs for the patties and mix with panko breadcrumbs and flour. Mix the halloumi and sweet potato into the egg mixture. Season with salt and pepper.
2. Cut the whole broccoli into smaller pieces.
3. Cook the quinoa following the instructions on the pack. When there is around 2 minutes of cooking time left, add the broccoli and put the lid on the pan.
4. Dollop 12 patties into a large, hot frying pan (skillet) with oil. Fry them for 3 minutes per side. Take them out and plate them.
5. Put the spinach and garlic in the frying pan and fry for a minute or so until the spinach wilts. Season with salt and pepper.
6. Fry the eggs in some oil in another frying pan.
7. Divide the quinoa and broccoli between the plates. Add the patties, spinach and fried eggs.

Vegan pizza with grilled pepper pesto

SERVES 4

800 g (1 lb 12 oz) pizza dough, preferably sourdough or homemade (page 177)

PAPRIKA PESTO

1 garlic clove, finely sliced

200 g (7 oz) tin grilled peppers

50 g (2 oz/½ cup) walnuts

1 teaspoon dried oregano

1 tablespoon white miso

½ tablespoon tomato purée (paste)

TOPPING

1 small courgette (zucchini)

8 blushing wood mushrooms or chestnut mushrooms

200 g (7 oz) vegesan (page 176)

mint leaves and lemon zest

salt and freshly ground black pepper

olive oil

This is a vegan pizza – so it doesn't contain any cheese. It's delicious – and something completely different to those regular pizzas, dripping in cheese. The miso gives the tomato sauce depth, but it's fine to skip it. On the other hand, vegesan or vegan cheese is necessary – otherwise the pizza will not only be flat in appearance but also flavour.

1. Preheat the oven to 240°C (475°F/Gas 9) and heat two baking trays.
2. Blitz the garlic, peppers, walnuts, oregano, miso and tomato purée into a pesto using a food processor or hand-held blender.
3. Roll or lay out the pizza dough on baking paper. Spread the pepper pesto onto it.
4. Slice the courgette and mushrooms thinly on top, preferably with a mandolin or cheese slicer. Sprinkle over half the vegesan and season with salt and pepper.
5. Remove the hot baking tray, add pizzas onto the hot baking trays and bake for 10–15 minutes until they take on colour.
6. Sprinkle the rest of the vegesan, the mint leaves and lemon zest on top. Brush lightly with olive oil.

Pizza bianco with mushrooms, Jerusalem artichokes and lemon

This is no pizza for a children's party – but is the kind you would serve to your adult friends. You might like to pour a glass of fizz and talk about life... Or just let the delicious pizza and its lemon aromas silence you.

SERVES 2

200 g (7 oz) Jerusalem artichokes

400 g (14 oz) pizza dough, preferably sourdough or homemade (page 177)

200 g (7 oz/¾ cup) crème fraîche

6 blushing wood mushrooms or chestnut mushrooms, sliced

3 tablespoons capers

8 sprigs of rosemary

230 g (8 oz) mozzarella

150 g (5 oz) Västerbotten cheese, grated

black pepper

rocket (arugula), lemon zest and olive oil for topping

TO SERVE

Fennel salad (page 157)

1. Preheat the oven to 250°C (480°F/Gas 9) and put a baking sheet into the oven to heat up.
2. Rinse the Jerusalem artichokes and slice them finely, preferably with a mandolin or cheese slicer.
3. Roll or lay out the pizza dough on a piece of baking paper.
4. Spread the crème fraîche on the dough. Add the Jerusalem artichoke slices, mushrooms, drained capers and rosemary leaves.
5. Tear the mozzarella into pieces and add them together with the cheese. Season with pepper.
6. Remove the hot baking tray, add the pizza and bake for around 10 minutes until the cheese has melted and the pizza has taken on colour.
7. Top with rocket, lemon zest and olive oil. Serve with fennel salad.

PIZZA SALAD

Tear any leftover pizza into smaller pieces and toast them in a hot oven or a frying pan (skillet) to form croutons. Mix with small leaf salad, grated mozzarella or burrata, halved cherry tomatoes and cooked lentils. Add a dressing made using balsamic vinegar, olive oil and honey. Add a little chilli flakes for an extra kick.

Falafel pizza with tomato chilli sauce and kale

If pizza had been invented in Israel rather than Italy, it might have looked a little like this. If you have time, make your own pizza bases and put them in the freezer. Defrost them as you heat the oven. You can double this recipe if there are lots of you eating.

400 g (14 oz) pizza dough, preferably sourdough or homemade (page 177)

200 g (7 oz/¾ cup) pre-prepared tomato sauce

1 teaspoon chilli flakes

1 teaspoon liquid honey

8 falafels, either fresh or defrosted from the freezer (page 175)

50 g (2 oz) Parmesan, grated

230 g (8 oz) mozzarella, grated

salt and freshly ground black pepper

75 g (2½ oz) kale

2 tablespoons tahini

3 tablespoons pine nuts

olive oil, to garnish

VEGAN

Flavour the tomato sauce with agave syrup instead of honey. Use vegan cheese or sprinkle vegesan (page 179) on top when the pizza comes out of the oven.

1. Preheat the oven to 250°C (480°F/Gas 9) and put a baking sheet into the oven to heat up.
2. Roll or lay out the pizza dough on baking paper.
3. Season the tomato sauce with chilli flakes and honey. Spread the sauce on the pizza dough. Halve the falafels and put on top. Cover with the Parmesan and mozzarella. Season with salt and pepper.
4. Remove the hot baking tray, add the pizza and bake for 5 minutes.
5. Shred the kale into small pieces. Put in a bowl and massage in the tahini. Season with salt.
6. Take the pizza out of the oven and add the kale and pine nuts. Bake for another 5 minutes until the kale is crispy and the pine nuts have taken on a little colour.
7. Drizzle with a little olive oil to finish.

Double taco with mashed black beans and taco-spiced sweet potato

SERVES 4

600 g (1 lb 5 oz) sweet potatoes

rapeseed (canola) oil

2 tablespoons taco seasoning (page 179)

2 avocados

75 g (2½ oz) feta, white cheese or Cheddar

salad leaves

8 soft mini tortillas, approximately 8 cm (3 in) in diameter.

8 hard taco shells

coriander (cilantro) leaves, to garnish

MASHED BLACK BEANS

1 large yellow onion, finely chopped

3 garlic cloves, finely chopped

1 green chilli, preferably jalapeño, seeded and finely chopped

2 teaspoons ground cumin

2 × 400 g (14 oz) tins pinto beans or black beans

1 teaspoon dried oregano

salt

zest and juice of ½ lime

rapeseed (canola) oil, for frying

VEGAN

Skip the cheese or use a vegan type.

I never thought I would write that I have been inspired by the American fast food chain Taco Bell, but they have a similar 'double-stacked taco' on their menu. The taco is very filling and uses just one type of taco, but it's delicious when you use both the soft tortillas and hard tacos. The amount of taco spice depends on whether you make your own or buy it in, as well as how you feel about hot food.

1. Preheat the oven to 220°C (430°F/Gas 8) and put in a baking tray.
2. Wash and slice the sweet potatoes into long, thin wedges (you don't need to peel them). Put them in a bowl and mix with a little oil and the taco spices. Place onto the hot baking tray and roast for 15–20 minutes until the wedges have taken on colour. Stir once while cooking. Season with salt, if desired.
3. To make the beans, fry the onion in oil in a saucepan for around 5 minutes over a medium-low heat until soft. Mix in the garlic, chilli and cumin and fry for 1 minute while stirring. Drain the beans, add them and the oregano and make sure everything is heated through.
4. Blend the beans in a food processor. Season with salt, lime zest and juice. Add water if the mixture ends up too thick.
5. Remove the stones from the avocados and then dice the flesh. Crumble or grate the cheese coarsely and divide the salad leaves.
6. Spread the mashed beans on the mini tortillas and then place them inside the taco shells. Fill with salad, sweet potato wedges and avocado, and then top with cheese. Garnish with coriander.

SERVES 4

4-8 corn tortilla wraps

smoked tortilla
chips (page 176)

80 g (3 oz) small leaf salad

sriracha or spicy tomato salsa

BEAN RICE

1 yellow onion, diced

olive oil, for frying

2 garlic cloves, finely chopped

200 g (7 oz/1 cup) brown
rice that cooks quickly,
or another rice

1 teaspoon dried oregano

2 teaspoons ground cumin

400 g (14 oz) tin
chopped tomatoes

250 ml (80 fl oz/1 cup) water

400 g (14 oz) tin kidney
beans, drained

5 tablespoons
nutritional yeast

salt and freshly ground
black pepper

AVOCADO AND COCONUT DRESSING

2 avocados

big bunch of coriander
(cilantro) leaves,
finely chopped

zest and juice of 1 lime

200 ml (7 fl oz/¾ cup)
coconut water or water

salt

Burrito with bean rice and avocado and coconut dressing

Whether it is an enchilada or a burrito depends on whether the tortilla is made with corn or wheat and if it is baked or not. Regardless of the grain and the baking, this is a filling wrap with an acidic avocado dressing made with coconut water. You can skip the smoked coconut chips, but they do give a great smoky flavour and a little bit of bite. I don't usually have spicy tomato salsa in – instead, I prefer to use sriracha. Without any sauce, the burrito is mild.

1. To make the rice, fry onion in oil in a saucepan over a medium-low heat for around 5 minutes until soft. Add the garlic, rice, herbs and spices and fry for another minute or so while stirring.

2. Mix in the tomatoes and water and cook according to the instructions on the rice pack until the rice is soft. Dilute with more water if it seems dry. Mix in the beans and nutritional yeast. Season with salt and pepper to taste.

3. To make the dressing, remove the stones from the avocados and mash the flesh. Then, mix with the coriander, including the stalks, the lime juice and the coconut water to form a smooth dressing. Season with lime zest and salt to taste.

4. Warm up the tortilla wraps in a dry frying pan (skillet) if you have time – this will make them even tastier.

5. Put the bean rice on the wraps and sprinkle the smoked coconut chips on top before rolling them up.

6. Serve the burrito with avocado dressing, salad and sriracha or spicy tomato salsa.

DOUBLE TACO WITH MASHED BLACK BEANS AND TACO-SPICED SWEET POTATO (PAGE 94)

BURRITO WITH BEAN RICE AND AVOCADO AND COCONUT DRESSING (PAGE 95)

CROWD PLEASERS

SERVES 4

300 g (10½ oz/5 cups)
panko breadcrumbs

100 g (3½ oz/¾ cup)
chickpea (gram) flour

90 g (3¼ oz/¾ cup) plain
(all-purpose) flour

¾ teaspoon salt

200 ml (7 fl oz/¾ cup) cold
beer or ice-cold water

200 g (7 oz) Portobello
or blushing wood
mushrooms, sliced

oil, for frying

RED CABBAGE SALAD

250 g (9 oz) red cabbage,
finely shredded

juice of ½ lime

1½ tablespoons maple syrup

1 tablespoon rice vinegar

big bunch of coriander
(cilantro) leaves

salad leaves, e.g. romaine
or crispy lettuce

CHIPOTLE SAUCE

100 g (3½ oz/⅓ cup) egg-free
mayonnaise (page 174)

3 tablespoons dairy-
free yoghurt

2 teaspoons chipotle paste

Beer-battered mushrooms with red cabbage salad and chipotle sauce

Smoked mayonnaise, crispy mushrooms and sweet and sour salad make for an incredible and grown-up vegan taco. I use salad leaves as tortillas, but if you're hungry it's fine to use both. The mushrooms get really crispy when dipped into a mixture of chickpea (gram) flour and plain (all-purpose) flour. The chickpea flour also provides great proteins, but it's fine to just use plain flour. Don't like mushrooms? Use avocado wedges instead.

1. To make the salad, mix the cabbage with the lime juice, syrup and vinegar, and massage for a minute or so until the cabbage softens. Chop the coriander, including the stalks. Save a little to garnish.
2. Mix together the ingredients for the chipotle sauce.
3. Put the panko breadcrumbs in a bowl.
4. Mix the two flours and salt in a separate bowl. Add the beer or ice-cold water and whisk into a smooth batter. Try dipping one mushroom to see whether the batter sticks. Add more plain flour if the batter is too thin, or more liquid if it is too thick.
5. Heat the oil.
6. Dip a few mushrooms at a time into the batter and then in the panko breadcrumbs. Put them in the oil and fry for 3–4 minutes until they have taken on colour all over and are crispy. Turn the pieces once while frying. Leave to drain on kitchen paper.
7. Put the red cabbage in the salad leaves (or the tortilla wraps), top with fried mushrooms and drizzle the chipotle sauce over the top or serve separately.

Lentil pancakes with spinach and goat's cheese salad

SERVES 4

400 g (14 oz) tin cooked lentils
or 300 g (10½ oz/
1½ cups) home-cooked lentils

3 eggs

600 ml (20 fl oz/2½ cups) milk

180 g (6½ oz/1½ cups)
plain (all-purpose) flour

salt

butter, for frying

HONEY YOGHURT

300 g (10½ fl oz/
1¼ cups) yoghurt

1 tablespoon liquid honey

SPINACH AND GOAT'S CHEESE SALAD

4 tablespoons smoked
almonds (page 176),
roughly chopped

80 g (3 oz) baby spinach

approximately 200 g
(7 oz) blueberries or
strawberries, or a
mix of the two

100 g (3½ oz) goat's cheese

2 tablespoons olive oil

2 teaspoons white
balsamic vinegar

salt and freshly ground
black pepper

Some children eat legumes quite happily. Others politely decline. These pancakes contain lentils but you don't have to tell them that since they're barely noticeable. At least if you use red lentils. Ready-cooked lentils work well, but I think you should use green lentils since tinned red lentils don't taste as good. If I have small visitors at my dinner table, I usually serve the pancakes with more blueberries. Children don't usually like spinach, but honey yoghurt and berries tend to go down a treat.

1. Drain the lentils if using tinned ones. Mix 200 g (7 oz/ 1 cup) of lentils with the eggs, milk and flour. Season with salt.
2. Fry the pancakes in butter using one or two warm frying pans (skillet).
3. In the meantime, mix the yoghurt with the honey.
4. Mix the almonds with the spinach, berries and the rest of the lentils. Break the goat's cheese into pieces and crumble it on top. Mix the olive oil, white balsamic vinegar, salt and freshly ground black pepper to form a dressing and pour over.
5. Serve the pancakes with the honey yoghurt and salad.

4

HELLO ASIA

---

*Delicious dishes with rice,
noodles and root vegetables*

One billion people can't be wrong. In Asia,
they have mastered cooking food with lots
of vegetables and proteins from the plant
kingdom. These dishes are tasty and often
vegan. Don't let the strong flavours or exotic
ingredients put you off. Most of them are
available in well-stocked supermarkets, but
if you can, you should shop in an Asian
specialist store. This usually ensures your
food tastes better and is cheaper.

600 g (1 lb 5 oz) french fries

salt and freshly ground
black pepper

400 g (14 oz) mushrooms,
e.g. oyster, blushing wood
or chestnut mushrooms

rapeseed (canola)
oil, for frying

1 garlic clove, finely chopped

300 g (10½ oz) pak choi (bok
choi), coarsely shredded

1 tablespoon Japanese
soy sauce

200 g (7 oz) silken tofu and
shredded spring onions
(scallions), to garnish

KIMCHI MAYONNAISE

100–200 g (3½–7 oz) Kimchi
(page 173), roughly chopped

100 g (3½/⅓ cup) Egg-free
mayonnaise (page 174)

Kimchi fries with mushrooms and pak choi

Frozen French fries aren't as bad for you as you might think, since you cook them in the oven. This is good, because it means you can add mayonnaise and eat them with a clear conscience. If you're not a vegan, you can swap the tofu for grated cheese and let it melt on top of the potatoes for a little extra indulgence. If you don't have any kimchi, you can flavour the rich mayonnaise with sriracha and lime zest.

1. Warm the oven and cook the French fries according to the instructions on the pack. Season with salt.
2. Rinse the mushrooms and tear or cut them into smaller pieces. Fry them in a frying pan (skillet) without fat for approximately 5 minutes over a high heat while stirring a little. Lower the heat, add a little oil and fry for another 5–10 minutes until the mushrooms have softened.
3. Mix the garlic and pak choi with the mushrooms and fry for another 2 minutes until the pak choi has softened. Add the soy sauce and season with pepper.
4. Roughly chop the kimchi and mix into the mayonnaise. The quantity of kimchi depends on its flavour and how strong you want the mayonnaise to be.
5. Serve the French fries with the mushroom mixture and kimchi mayonnaise. Crumble the tofu on top and garnish with spring onions.

KIMCHI QUESADILLA

If you have any mushrooms leftover, make quesadillas. Spread egg-free mayonnaise (or normal mayonnaise if you're not vegan) on tortilla wraps and then layer the mushroom mixture and grated cheese on top. Fold together and fry in a frying pan (skillet) until the cheese melts. It doesn't matter if a few fries sneak in!

Vietnamese peanut rice and lemongrass tofu

SERVES 4

300 g (10½ oz/1½ cups) jasmine rice

100 g (3½ oz/⅔ cup) peanuts, preferably unsalted

1 tablespoon sugar

¾ teaspoon salt

LEMONGRASS TOFU

400 g (14 oz) firm tofu

3 lemongrass stalks

2 garlic cloves, finely chopped

1 red chilli, seeded and finely chopped

3 tablespoons Japanese soy sauce

juice of ½ lime

1 tablespoon sugar

2 tablespoons water

1 tablespoon sesame oil

rapeseed (canola) oil, for frying

SALAD

fresh herbs, preferably coriander (cilantro), mint and Thai basil leaves

1 large carrot, peeled and grated

80 g (3 oz) tender salad leaves

lime wedges, to serve

When I think of Vietnamese food, it's fresh herbs that spring to mind. The coriander (cilantro) in this dish is essential, but ideally you should get all three herbs – they're well worth it. Life is full of choices, and so is this recipe. For instance, you can add steamed broccoli or pak choi (bok choi), or have it with noodles instead of rice.

1. Cut the tofu into 5 mm (¼ in) thin slices and put in a bowl.
2. Remove the outer leaves and slice the lemongrass lengthways. Hit the stalks with the handle of a knife and then chop them finely. Mix the garlic and chilli with the soy sauce to form a marinade and pour over the tofu.
3. Cook the rice without salt, following the instructions on the pack.
4. Rinse the peanuts if you are using salted nuts. Finely chop them and mix with the sugar and salt.
5. Pluck the herb leaves from the plants and mix them with the carrot and salad mixture.
6. Fry the tofu in rapeseed oil in a frying pan (skillet). Take out the pieces and plate them. Pour any remaining marinade into the pan. Add the lime juice, sugar, water and sesame oil.
7. Mix the peanut sprinkles with the rice.
8. Top the rice with the tofu, the sauce from the pan and the salad. Serve with lime wedges.

300 g (10½ oz/1½ cups) rice, preferably wholegrain or quick cook brown rice

300 g (10½ oz) frozen soybeans, defrosted

2 avocados

200 g (7 oz) alfalfa sprouts or other sprouts

furikake (page 179) or roasted sesame seeds

GINGER-MARINATED MELON

40 g (1½ oz) ginger

1 teaspoon agave syrup

1 tablespoon rice vinegar

2 tablespoons Japanese soy sauce

700 g (1 lb 9 oz) watermelon, diced

MISO MAYONNAISE

zest and juice of ½ lime

150 g (5 oz/⅔ cup) egg-free mayonnaise (page 174)

1 tablespoon white miso

salt, agave syrup and sriracha (optional)

Rice bowl with miso mayonnaise and ginger-marinated melon

It has been popular for some time to serve things in bowls – but truth be told the food is just as tasty when served on a plate. When watermelon season is over, you can use radishes or kohlrabi instead. Or why not all three? If you like your food a little hotter, flavour the miso mayonnaise with sriracha.

1. Cook the rice following the instructions on the pack.
2. To prepare the melon, peel and finely grate the ginger, squeeze out the juice and discard the remains. Mix the ginger juice, syrup, vinegar and soy sauce, and pour over the melon. The quantity of syrup will depend on how sweet your melon is, so do taste a little first. Leave in the fridge.
3. Mix the ingredients for the mayonnaise. Season with salt and agave syrup, and sriracha if you like.
4. Add the soybeans to the top of the saucepan with the rice so that they warm up.
5. Remove the stones from the avocados and slice the flesh.
6. Put the rice and soybeans into the bottom of a bowl or on a plate, and then put the watermelon and avocado slices on top. Top with alfalfa sprouts and furikake or sesame seeds. Serve with the miso mayonnaise.

FRIED CURRY RICE WITH FRIED SALAD AND EGGS

If there's leftover rice, you can make fried rice. Finely chop some spring onions (scallions) and fry in a little curry powder. Add the cooked rice and season with Japanese soy sauce. Fry an egg in a separate frying pan (skillet). Divide a head of lettuce, like a romaine, into quarters and fry with the cut side down. Top the curry rice with salad, eggs, crispy onions and sriracha.

Mushroom bibimbap with kimchi and eggs

The Koreans love bibimbap, which is made using rice and shredded vegetables positioned in symmetrical heaps. This is my speedy Western version – not quite as good-looking but definitely just as tasty. Bibim means 'to mix' and bap means 'rice'. The mixing takes place at the table just before you eat. The bibimbap can be served with fried eggs, poached eggs, or even just raw egg yolks.

1. Cook the rice following the instructions on the pack.
2. Tear the mushrooms into pieces or slice them finely. Fry them in a dry frying pan (skillet) for around 5 minutes until they take on some colour. Stir occasionally. Lower the heat, add a little oil and fry for another 5–10 minutes until the mushrooms have softened.
3. In the meantime, mix the ingredients for the dressing.
4. Thinly slice the cucumber, preferably with a mandolin or cheese slicer. Pour half of the dressing over the cucumber.
5. Fry the eggs in a separate frying pan.
6. Put the mushroom mixture together with the spinach and garlic. Fry for a minute or so until the spinach has softened. Pour the rest of the dressing over it.
7. Position the mushrooms, cucumber and kimchi in piles on top of the rice. Add the eggs. Top with furikake or toasted sesame seeds and sriracha or gochurang paste.

SERVES 4

300 g (10½ oz/1½ cups) rice, e.g. basmati or brown rice

400 g (14 oz) oyster mushrooms or 250 g (9 oz) blushing wood mushrooms or chestnut mushrooms

rapeseed (canola) oil, for frying

1 small cucumber

4 eggs

140 g (4½ oz) baby spinach

1 garlic clove, finely chopped

200 g (7 oz) kimchi or sauerkraut kimchi (page 173)

furikake (page 179) or roasted sesame seeds

sriracha or gochujang paste, mixed with water and sesame oil

SOY DRESSING

3 tablespoons Japanese soy sauce

2 tablespoons sesame oil

2 tablespoons rice vinegar

2 tablespoons liquid honey

VEGAN

Skip the eggs and use agave syrup instead of honey. Top with a little crumbled silken tofu.

RICE BOWL WITH MISO MAYONNAISE AND GINGER-MARINATED MELON (PAGE 108)

Tandoori-roasted cauliflower with lentil rice

Tandoors are a type of clay oven. Here I let the spices give flavour to the cauliflower, which is then roasted in a normal oven. Great with coconut rice with crispy lentils and nut and chilli sprinkles. If you don't shake the tin, the coconut cream and water will separate. But it doesn't matter if they get mixed up, it's just that the coconut cream is harder to whisk. Don't be too distraught if you happen to burn the rice a little. Scrape the crispy rice from the bottom of the saucepan and eat it – it's delicious.

SERVES 4

400 g (14 oz) tin coconut cream

200 g (7 oz/1 cup) basmati rice

1 teaspoon turmeric

salt

800 g (1 lb 12 oz) cauliflower

1½ tablespoons tandoori spice

rapeseed (canola) oil

1 lime

200 g (7 oz/1 cup) cooked green lentils

NUT AND CHILLI SPRINKLES

100 g (3½ oz/⅔ cup) salted and roasted cashews, roughly chopped

big bunch of coriander (cilantro) leaves, shredded

1 red chilli, seeded and finely chopped

1. Preheat the oven to 220°C (430°F/Gas 8) and put in a baking tray.
2. Remove the thick coconut cream from the tin and put it in a bowl. Measure out the thinner coconut water and put it in a saucepan. Fill with water so that the total volume of liquid corresponds with the cooking instructions on the rice packet. Add the rice and turmeric, and season with salt. Cook the rice according to its instructions.
3. Remove the green leaves from the cauliflower and put them in a pan. Break the remainder of the cauliflower into small florets or cut into pieces. Put them in a separate bowl, season with tandoori spice and salt, and drizzle oil on top. Put the cauliflower pieces on the warm tray and oven roast for 10 minutes.
4. Mix the green cauliflower leaves with a little oil. Put them on the tray and roast for a further 5–10 minutes until they have taken on some colour.
5. Cut half the lime into wedges. Zest the other half and squeeze out the juice. Whisk the remaining coconut cream until firm and add the lime juice and zest. Season with salt.
6. Mix the cashews, coriander and chilli together. Mix the coconut rice with the lentils.
7. Serve the cauliflower with the rice, drizzle the lime cream on top and finish off with the nut and chilli sprinkles. Serve with lime wedges.

RICE PATTIES WITH LENTILS

Mix any leftover rice with whisked egg, finely chopped chilli and coriander (cilantro). Season with some Indian spices, crumbled feta and cooked lentils. Form into small patties and turn them in panko breadcrumbs. Fry the patties in oil until crispy. Serve with steamed vegetables and yoghurt flavoured with ginger.

Cauliflower in sweet and sour sauce with sesame rice

These roasted chunks of cauliflower are sweet, hot and sticky. They're reminiscent of fried food served in Chinese restaurants in the West, even if they're not as crispy. But I'm glad to escape both the prawns and the oil. The toasted nuts give the rice a good, nutty flavour and lots of healthy vitamins and antioxidants to boot.

SERVES 4

300 g (10½ oz/1½ cups) rice (any type)

800 g (1 lb 12 oz) cauliflower

165 g (5½ oz/1⅓ cups) plain (all-purpose) flour

½ teaspoon salt

250 ml (8½ oz/1 cup) ice-cold water

100 g (3½ oz/1⅔ cups) panko breadcrumbs

rapeseed (canola) oil, for frying

100 g (3½ oz/⅔ cup) mixed seeds, e.g. sesame, sunflower or flaxseeds

spring onions (scallions), finely chopped, to garnish

SWEET AND SOUR SAUCE

40 g (1½ oz) ginger

2 garlic cloves, finely chopped

rapeseed (canola) oil, for frying

1 tablespoon rice vinegar

1 tablespoon tomato purée (paste)

3 tablespoons Japanese soy sauce

4 tablespoons sugar

1 teaspoon sriracha

1. Preheat the oven to 220°C (430°F/Gas 8).
2. Cook the rice following the instructions on the pack.
3. Remove the green leaves from the cauliflower and put them in a pan. Break the remainder of the cauliflower into small florets or cut into pieces.
4. Whisk the flour, salt and water in a bowl. The mixture should be fairly firm, so add more flour if it doesn't stick to the cauliflower. Dip a few pieces of cauliflower at a time into the flour mixture, and then place them on a greased baking tray. Sprinkle panko breadcrumbs on top and oven roast the cauliflower chunks for 10 minutes.
5. To make the sauce, peel and grate the ginger. Squeeze the juice and discard the remains. Fry the garlic in a little oil in a saucepan for around 1 minute while stirring. Add the rest of the sauce ingredients and simmer for approximately 5 minutes until it takes on a fairly syrupy consistency. Dilute with water if the sauce gets too thick.
6. Mix the cauliflower leaves with oil. Turn the cauliflower pieces on the tray and place the leaves beside them. Roast for a further 10 minutes.
7. Toast the seeds in a dry frying pan (skillet) without fat and mix them with the rice.
8. Pour the sauce over the cauliflower and sprinkle with the spring onions.

CRISPY RICE CAKES WITH WITH SPINACH AND EGG

Pour plenty of oil into a frying pan (skillet). Spread out any leftover rice in the pan and fry for around 10 minutes over a high heat until the rice is crisp on the bottom. Put a lid on the pan, lower the heat and fry for another 2 minutes until the whole rice patty is warm. In the meantime, fry an egg in a separate frying pan. Mix in a little spinach and let it soften. Season with salt. Top the rice patty with eggs, spinach and hoisin sauce or sriracha. Or even both!

TANDOORI-COOKED CAULIFLOWER WITH LENTIL RICE (PAGE 112)

CAULIFLOWER IN SWEET AND SOUR SAUCE WITH SESAME RICE (PAGE 113)

Crispy tofu with noodles and hoisin sauce in salad leaves

100 g (3½ oz) glass noodles

2 pots of coriander (cilantro) leaves

100 g (3½ oz/⅔ cup) salted peanuts, chopped

2 carrots, peeled and grated

150 g (5 oz) sugar snap peas, shredded

2 tablespoons hoisin sauce

1 tablespoon sesame oil

1 romaine or cosmopolitan lettuce, to serve

hoisin and sriracha, to serve

CRISPY TOFU

400 g (14 oz) firm tofu

4 tablespoons cornflour (cornstarch) and ½ teaspoon salt

rapeseed (canola) oil, for deep-frying

1 teaspoon five spice

1 teaspoon black pepper

½ teaspoon salt

Small, crispy salad packages with filling noodles, crispy tofu and the mild flavour of Chinese hoisin sauce. Often, the quality of the sauce varies, which makes life a little complicated. The sauce you can buy in Asian stores tastes good but is quite thick. Hoisin sauces from supermarkets have a good consistency but often need to be seasoned with sugar, lime juice and soy sauce. Try a few different brands until you find your favourite. If you can't find five spice, you can skip this or make your own.

1. Cook the noodles following the instructions on the pack. Rinse in cold water.
2. Chop the coriander, including the stalks. Save some coriander to garnish. Mix half the nuts with the coriander, carrots, sugar snap peas, the hoisin sauce, the noodles and sesame oil.
3. Cube the tofu and dry it using kitchen paper so that most of the moisture disappears. Season with salt and coat in cornstarch.
4. Heat up plenty of oil in a large frying pan (skillet) and deep fry the tofu in batches, a few minutes per side, until it is crispy. Mix the five spice, black pepper and salt, and sprinkle the mixture on the tofu.
5. Pull apart the salad leaves and place them on a large plate. Put the noodles in the salad leaves. Top with tofu and the rest of the nuts. Serve with hoisin sauce and sriracha.

SERVES 4

300 g (10½ oz/½ cups) rice,
preferably wholegrain rice

2 tablespoons sesame seeds

250 g (9 oz) broccoli
(or broccolini)

150 g (5 oz) haricots verts

sesame oil

AUBERGINE IN BLACK BEAN SAUCE

400 g (14 oz) aubergine
(eggplant), diced

rapeseed (canola)
oil, for frying

3 garlic cloves, finely sliced

300 g (10½ oz) firm tofu, diced

1 red chilli, deseeded
and sliced

4 tablespoons black
bean sauce/paste

1 tablespoon red wine vinegar

2 tablespoons sugar

200 ml (7 fl oz/¾ cup) water

black pepper

Aubergine in black bean sauce with broccoli and haricots verts

When you are far from China, or even your nearest Chinese restaurant, you have to step up to the plate. If you don't like tofu, you can fry mushrooms and boil soybeans instead to make sure you get plenty of protein. If you like, you can stir-fry all the vegetables, but it'll be a squeeze in wok, and I like the contrast between the soft umami-flavoured aubergine and the crunchy cooked vegetables.

1. Cook the rice following the instructions on the pack.
2. Toast the sesame seeds in a dry frying pan (skillet) without any fat. Stir them occasionally, as they burn easily. Remove the seeds from the frying pan and put to one side.
3. Fry the aubergine without fat in a frying pan for approximately 5 minutes until it has taken on a fine, almost black colour on the outer surface. Stir occasionally. Add a little rapeseed oil, reduce the heat and fry for another 5 minutes or so until the aubergine is soft.
4. Heat a saucepan of salted water for the broccoli and haricots verts.
5. Divide the broccoli into florets. Peel the stalk and cut it into smaller pieces. Clean the haricots verts.
6. Mix the garlic, tofu and chilli in the frying pan with the aubergine and fry for another minute or so until the tofu has taken on some colour.
7. Add the bean sauce/paste, vinegar, sugar and water. Stir and let the sauce simmer for a minute or so. Season with black pepper and more sugar if necessary.
8. Cook the broccoli and haricots verts until al dente. Drain them and mix with a little sesame oil.
9. Serve the rice with the aubergine, vegetables and toasted sesame seeds.

HELLO ASIA

Okonomiyaki with avocado

This Japanese dish lies in the borderlands between pancakes and frittata. Yaki means 'grilled' and okonomi means 'done your way'. I want mine with lots of greenery, so I serve it alongside avocado and salad. It's tricky barbecuing indoors, but using a grill pan or two is fine. In Japan, the dish is often served with mayonnaise and a special okonomiyaki sauce, but if you want a slightly healthier topping, you can try pickled ginger – gari – and yoghurt flavoured with wasabi.

SERVES 2

300 g (10½ oz) pointed cabbage or tender white cabbage

100 g (3½ oz) leeks or spring onions (scallions)

1½ tablespoons white miso

3 eggs

150 ml (5 fl oz/⅔ cup) cold water

90 g (3¼ oz/¾ cups) plain (all-purpose) flour

100 g (3½ oz/1⅔ cups) panko breadcrumbs

oil, for frying

BBQ SAUCE WITH SESAME OIL

4 tablespoons barbecue sauce

2 tablespoons ketchup

1 teaspoon sesame oil

2 teaspoons honey

ACCOMPANIMENTS

1 avocado

4 tablespoons mayonnaise, plus sugar and water

80 g (3 oz) tender salad leaves

1. Preheat the oven to 180°C (350°F/Gas 4).
2. Finely shred the cabbage and rinse. Then, finely shred the leek or spring onions.
3. Mix the miso, eggs and water in a bowl. Add the flour and whisk into a smooth batter. Then add the cabbage, leek/spring onion and panko breadcrumbs.
4. Heat up one or two frying pans (skillets) with oil and add half of the batter. Even out and spread the batter around so that the cabbage at the edges doesn't burn easily and so the pancake is round. Fry for approximately 5 minutes over a medium heat, preferably under a lid, until the cabbage has taken on colour and the pancake has solidified somewhat. Turn over and fry for 5 minutes on the other side until the pancake is solid and has taken on colour. If you think it's difficult to turn the pancake, use two spatulas and a plate – or even another frying pan.
5. Keep the okonomiyaki warm in the oven. Repeat with the rest of the batter.
6. Remove the stone from the avocado and slice it thinly.
7. Mix the mayonnaise with a pinch of sugar and a little water so that it can be drizzled.
8. Mix the ingredients for the sauce. The quantity of honey depends on how sweet your barbecue sauce is.
9. Drizzle mayonnaise and sauce over the okonomiyaki. Top with avocado slices and salad leaves.

Indian vegetable fritters with mango chutney dip

Pakora, pakoda, bhaji or fritters? These fried delights have many names. Regardless of what they're called, these tasty morsels are served throughout India, often as snacks between meals. With rice, salad and yoghurt on the plate, you can also serve them as a main course. I've chosen vegetables that can be shredded quickly, but you could just as well use potatoes, sweet potatoes, pumpkin, peppers and carrots, etc. The important thing is that the vegetables are shredded to about the same size.

300 g (10½ oz/1½ cups)
rice (any type)

1 lime

300 g (10½ oz/1¼ cups) yoghurt

3 tablespoons mango chutney

80 g (3 oz) mixed salad leaves

salt

coriander (cilantro)
leaves, to garnish

PAKORA

200 g (7 oz) white cabbage

¾ teaspoon salt

1 teaspoon garam
masala spice mix

300 g (10½ oz/2½ cups)
chickpea (gram) flour

200 ml (7 fl oz/¾ cup)
cold water

3 silverskin onions,
finely sliced

1–2 green chillies, halved
and finely sliced

oil, for frying

VEGAN

Use dairy-free yoghurt.

1. Cook the rice following the instructions on the pack.
2. Finely shred the white cabbage and cut it into smaller pieces.
3. Mix the salt, garam masala and chickpea flour in a large bowl. Add the water and whisk into a firm batter.
4. Add the onion, cabbage and chilli (only use one chilli, or deseed the chilli if you don't like hot food) to the batter and mix thoroughly. Add more flour to the batter if it is too loose or more water if it is too thick, but remember that the vegetables will release some water.
5. Heat up oil in a large saucepan.
6. Halve the lime and cut one half into wedges. Zest the other half and squeeze out the juice. Mix the yoghurt, mango chutney, lime juice and zest. Season with salt and put in the fridge.
7. Dollop 2 tablespoons of batter into the hot oil and fry in batches, approximately 3 minutes per pakora. Take out of the oil and leave to drain on kitchen paper.
8. Serve with the rice, mango chutney dip and salad leaves. Garnish with lime wedges and coriander.

Malaysian noodles with tofu and white cabbage

Char kway teow is a Malaysian rice noodle dish that is, in my view, just as delicious as Thailand's pad thai. This is a vegan version with curry powder and Japanese miso, instead of the Malaysian prawn paste that is usually included. I have borrowed one thing from the Thais – I serve them with white cabbage wedges, chilli flakes and lime. If you eat eggs, you can fry one to serve alongside.

SERVES 4

250 g (9 oz) noodles, preferably wide rice noodles

100 g (3½ oz) spring onions (scallions)

300 g (10½ oz) cabbage

300 g (10½ oz) tofu, diced

rapeseed (canola) oil, for frying

3 garlic cloves, finely chopped

200 g (7 oz) beansprouts

75 ml (2½ fl oz/⅓ cup) water

crispy onions, chilli flakes and lime wedges, to serve

WOK SAUCE

1 teaspoon sugar

2 teaspoons curry powder

1 tablespoon Japanese soy sauce

1 tablespoon white miso

1 tablespoon sesame oil

3 tablespoons sweet soy sauce (ketjap manis)

1. Cook the noodles al dente following the instructions on the pack. Rinse in cold water.
2. Whisk together all the wok sauce ingredients.
3. Shred the spring onions. Put aside one quarter for serving. Cut the white cabbage into four wedges.
4. Fry the tofu in a little rapeseed oil for approximately 3 minutes in a large frying pan (skillet) or wok. If you don't have a large frying pan, it's best to divide the recipe in two and fry in batches. Mix in the garlic, beansprouts and spring onions. Add the noodles, wok sauce and water. Ensure everything is heated through.
5. Serve the noodles with the white cabbage and lime wedges, as well as crispy onions, chilli flakes and the remainder of the spring onions.

Gado-gado with peanut sauce and eggs

Gado-gado is an Indonesian dish where warm peanut butter is poured over cooked vegetables. I love a little crispiness, which is why I don't cook the carrots and sprouts. Including potatoes is a given – as far as the Indonesians and I are concerned – but apart from that, you can choose any vegetables. Spend a few extra pennies and select a good potato variety. Fried tofu or tempeh is well worth it if you want extra protein.

SERVES 4

600 g (1 lb 5 oz) potatoes

4 eggs

2 carrots

300 g (10½ oz) fresh beans,
e.g. haricot (navy), or
mangetout (snow peas)

150 g (5 oz) beansprouts

green salad or gem lettuce

crispy onions and
toasted coconut chips

salt

PEANUT SAUCE

2 garlic cloves

rapeseed (canola)
oil, for frying

½ teaspoon sambal oelek

200 g (7 oz) peanut butter,
preferably crunchy

150 ml (5 fl oz/⅔ cup)
coconut cream

juice of ½ lime

2 teaspoons sweet soy
sauce (ketjap manis)

100 ml (3½ fl oz/½ cup) water

VEGAN

Skip the eggs and use
fried tofu instead.

1. Wash the potatoes. Cook them until soft in salted water for approximately 20 minutes.
2. Soft boil the eggs for 6–7 minutes. Peel them and halve them once they have cooled somewhat.
3. Peel and finely chop the garlic cloves for the peanut sauce. Fry the garlic in oil for approximately 30 seconds in a saucepan until soft. Add the sambal oelek and fry for another 30 seconds. Add the other ingredients and leave to simmer. Add the water to achieve the desired consistency.
4. Peel and grate or shred the carrots, preferably using a potato peeler.
5. Cut the beans diagonally into pieces, and put them in the potato water when there is around a minute left of cooking time.
6. Divide the salad and vegetables across the plates. Pour over the sauce and top with eggs, crispy onions and coconut chips.

CRISPY POTATO AND ASPARAGUS PIE

Brush about six sheets of filo pastry with melted butter. Spread herb-flavoured fresh cheese on top to cover it all, add sliced potatoes, pieces of asparagus and mature grated cheese. Season with salt and freshly ground black pepper. Bake at 22°C (430°F/Gas 8) in the oven for 15–20 minutes until the pie is golden.

2 stalks of lemongrass

1 garlic clove, finely chopped

1 teaspoon five spice
or ground cumin

3 tablespoons Japanese
soy sauce

500 g (1 lb 2 oz) tofu, sliced

5 tablespoons cornflour
(cornstarch)

rapeseed (canola)
oil, for frying

QUICK-PICKLED CARROTS

4 tablespoons rice vinegar

2 tablespoons agave syrup

2 pinches of salt

1 tablespoon water

2 carrots

CHILLI MAYONNAISE

100 g (3½ oz/⅓ cup) egg-free
mayonnaise (page 174)

1–2 teaspoons sriracha

TO SERVE

2 baguettes or
8 mini baguettes

100 g (3½ oz) peanut butter,
preferably crunchy

salad leaves

coriander (cilantro) leaves

crispy onions

Báhn mì with peanut butter

The French left behind plenty of exciting culinary heritage in Vietnam, including crème caramel and baguettes. For that, we say merci and make the Vietnamese báhn mì sandwich, but vegan-style using tofu and peanut butter. If you're looking for a burger rather than a sandwich, you put it all in a sourdough burger bun. Steaming edamame beans are a great side to this dish.

1. Remove the outer leaves and cut the lemongrass lengthways. Hit the stalks with the handle of a knife and then chop them finely. Mix the lemongrass, garlic, five spice or cumin and soy sauce to form a marinade. Put the tofu slices on a plate and pour over the marinade. Leave to marinade while you prepare everything else.

2. Boil the rice vinegar, syrup, salt and water. Peel and finely shred or grate the carrots, ideally by using a mandolin, cheese slicer or potato peeler. Put the slices in the vinegar mixture and leave to cool.

3. Mix the ingredients for the mayonnaise.

4. Slice the bread and spread with peanut butter.

5. Pat the tofu slices dry and coat them in cornflour. Fry in plenty of oil until crispy.

6. Put the salad leaves, tofu, pickled carrots, coriander and crispy onions onto the bread. Drizzle the sauce on top.

5

GREEN IS GOOD

Filling salads and green sides

When you're craving salad and your kids or better half scream no, you can do one of two things: you can either give up and fry meatballs or you can try to figure out why they are objecting so loudly. Perhaps they think it won't be filling enough? Perhaps they don't like it when everything is mixed together in a giant heap? But if you make the salad filling and put everything into separate piles, even the most discerning guests usually enjoy eating it.

Roasted quinoa with feta and pear

Quinoa is a really healthy little seed filled with proteins and vitamins. I don't love the flavour, but I've been practising for a while and have concluded that roasted quinoa is delicious. Quinoa contains saponins, a bitter substance that has to be rinsed away, which is sometimes done before you buy it. When you tire of feta, you can use goat's cheese, Parmesan or blue cheese instead.

SERVES 4

200 g (7 oz/1 cup) quinoa

2 beetroots (beets), peeled and grated

500 ml (17 fl oz/2 cups) water

1 avocado

2 pears

150 g (5 oz) feta

80 g (3 oz) rocket (arugula) or mixed leaves with rocket

salt and freshly ground black pepper

olive oil, to serve

TOASTED ROSEMARY ALMONDS

75 g (2½ oz/½ cup) blanched almonds

3 sprigs of rosemary

1 tablespoon liquid honey

rock salt

VEGAN

Use agave syrup instead of honey. Sprinkle vegan cheese and salad seed sprinkles on top (page 178).

1. Roast the quinoa in a dry, high-sided frying pan (skillet) over a high heat for approximately 5 minutes until the seeds begin to pop, take on a brown colour and smell nutty. Stir constantly.
2. Pour the quinoa into a sieve and rinse them to remove the unhealthy bitter substances. If it has been pre-rinsed you don't have to do this.
3. Cook the quinoa and grated beetroot in salted water for approximately 15 minutes until they are soft. Stir once while cooking. Add more water if it boils off.
4. Toast the almonds and rosemary in a dry frying pan (skillet) without any fat. Stir in the honey. Plate up and sprinkle with rock salt. Roughly chop the almonds once they have cooled somewhat.
5. Remove the stone from the avocado and slice the flesh into pieces. Then, slice the pears and crumble over the cheese.
6. Put the rocket on a plate and then add the other ingredients. Drizzle with a little olive oil and season with black pepper.

QUINOA PATTIES WITH BEETROOT

Mix any leftover quinoa
with whisked egg and a little
chickpea (gram) flour or oats.
Add finely grated, squeezed
beetroots and crumbled cheese.
Season with salt, pepper, thyme
and lemon zest. Shape into
small patties. Leave the patties
to rest in the fridge/freezer if
not cooking immediately, and
then fry in oil.

Rye salad with roasted broccoli and burrata

A salad for dinner can be filling, crispy, flavourful and absolutely wonderful. This is a warm version with both roasted and raw vegetables, and the creamy Italian cheese burrata – made using mozzarella and cream. If you don't have time to make your own smoked almonds, you can buy tamari-roasted or smoked ones from the shops, or you can use ordinary almonds. The smoky version is good, but sometimes you have to make do with just the texture.

SERVES 4

200 g (7 oz/1 cup) rye, farro or another wheat mix

250 g (9 oz) broccoli

2 tablespoons olive oil

salt and freshly ground black pepper

400 g (14 oz) cherry tomatoes, preferably on the vine

60 g (2 oz) rocket (arugula)

75 g (2½ oz/½ cup) smoked almonds (page 176), roughly chopped

75 g (2½ oz) Parmesan, grated

230 g (8 oz) burrata or mozzarella

big bunch of basil leaves, to garnish

HONEY VINAIGRETTE

4 tablespoons olive oil

2 tablespoons white balsamic vinegar

1 teaspoon honey

salt and freshly ground black pepper

chilli flakes

1. Preheat the oven to 220°C (430°F/Gas 8) and put in a baking tray.
2. Cook the wheat following the instructions on the pack.
3. Cut the broccoli into pieces and put in a bowl, pour on olive oil and season with salt and pepper. Take the hot tray out of the oven, line with baking paper and distribute the broccoli on top. Place the tomatoes on the tray and roast for approximately 15 minutes until the broccoli and tomatoes have taken on colour. You may need to remove the broccoli while roasting the tomatoes for a further 5 minutes.
4. Mix the olive oil, vinegar and honey for the dressing. Season with salt, black pepper and chilli flakes.
5. Put the rocket on a plate. Mix the wheat, broccoli and tomatoes, and put on top together with the burrata. Pour the dressing over it and top with Parmesan, almonds and fresh basil.

VEGAN

Use agave syrup instead of honey. Sprinkle vegesan (page 179) on top instead of Parmesan and burrata, and serve with artichokes with cannellini beans (page 161).

150 g (5 oz/¾ cup)
uncooked green lentils

1 cucumber, peeled
and seeded

2 pitta breads or 2 slices
of multigrain bread

olive oil, for frying

400 g (14 oz) cherry
tomatoes, chopped

75 g (2½ oz) spring onions
(scallions), chopped

big bunch of flat-leaf
parsley, roughly chopped

big bunch of mint leaves,
roughly chopped

1 romaine or crispy
lettuce, shredded

dukkah (page 178) or roasted
sesame seeds, to serve

DRESSING

4 tablespoons olive oil

2 tablespoons
pomegranate syrup

salt and freshly ground
black pepper

Bread salad with green lentils

Fattousch is a salad from the Middle East with fried pitta bread. In Italy, bread salads are made using multigrain bread and are called panzanella. This salad is a mixture of the two and features protein-rich lentils. So don't throw away dry bread. Tear or cut it into pieces instead, and put it in the freezer as it's perfect for getting out on occasions like this for use in salads. The seed, nut and spice mix known as dukkah from the Middle East provides extra texture and flavour, but you can also use sesame seeds. If you don't have pomegranate syrup, you can make a normal vinaigrette.

1. Cook the lentils following the instructions on the pack.
2. Cut the cucumber into semi-circles.
3. Mix olive oil and pomegranate syrup for the dressing. Season with salt and pepper to taste.
4. Tear the bread into pieces and fry in oil until golden.
5. Mix the lentils with the dressing, tomatoes, cucumber, spring onions and herbs. Put the salad on a plate. Add the lentils and pieces of bread, as well as the dukkah or sesame seeds.

RYE SALAD WITH ROASTED BROCCOLI AND BURRATA (PAGE 134)

BREAD SALAD WITH GREEN LENTILS (PAGE 135)

Grazing platter with lemon-marinated fennel and halloumi

This is the only type of salad my kids like. Probably because they can see what they're eating since halloumi is a family favourite and because the salad contains fruit. I usually keep back the fennel just for myself, so I tend to flavour it with both fennel seeds and chilli. If the kids are left to choose, the salad gets topped with a big dollop of high-fat yoghurt (I prefer tzatziki).

SERVES 4

200 g (7 oz/1 cup) bulgur

a pinch of saffron or
1 teaspoon turmeric

1 cucumber, peeled
and seeded

500 g (1 lb 2 oz) watermelon

1 head of lettuce

200 g (7 oz) pomegranate
seeds, preferably frozen

200 g (7 oz) halloumi

olive oil, for frying

3 tablespoons salad
seed sprinkles (page
178) or other seeds

LEMON-MARINATED FENNEL

1 fennel bulb

3 tablespoons olive oil

zest and juice of ½ lemon

1 teaspoon liquid honey

½ teaspoon chilli flakes

1 teaspoon fennel seed

salt and freshly ground
black pepper

VEGAN

Skip the halloumi and
serve with falafel. Flavour
the dressing with agave
syrup instead of honey.

1. Cook the bulgur with saffron or turmeric according to the instructions on the pack.
2. Thinly slice the fennel. Mix all the other ingredients for the lemon marinade. Season with salt and pepper and pour over the fennel.
3. Cut the cucumber into semi-circles.
4. Slice the watermelon and divide the lettuce into smaller leaves.
5. Put everything, including the pomegranate seeds, in heaps on a plate.
6. Slice the halloumi, fry it in oil until golden, then put it on top together with the seeds.

GREEN IS GOOD

250 g (9 oz) soba noodles

1 cucumber

1 unripe mango

big bunch of coriander
(cilantro) leaves

big bunch of mint or
Thai basil leaves

150 g (5 oz) beansprouts

75 g (2½ oz/½ cup) salted
peanuts or cashews, chopped

1 head of salad, e.g.
romaine or crispy lettuce

4 tablespoons toasted
coconut chips, to garnish

LIME DRESSING WITH GINGER

1 red chilli

40 g (1½ oz) ginger

1 lime

2 tablespoons olive oil

1 tablespoon Japanese
soy sauce

1 tablespoon sesame oil

2 teaspoons agave syrup

Noodle salad with unripened mango and cashews

Unripened mango has an almost acrid flavour, but offers great texture. It's best sliced thinly and added to salads with a sweet and sour dressing. If you have a sweet tooth, you can swap it for ripe mango, and if you don't like fruit then kohlrabi also works well. Soba noodles are Japanese noodles made using protein-rich buckwheat. These often also contain plain flour, so if you're a coeliac you should double check the list of ingredients on the packaging.

1. Cook the noodles following the instructions on the pack.
2. Peel, deseed and slice the cucumber. Peel the mango and continue to peel the flesh into thin slices, or grate it coarsely using a grater. Chop the coriander, including the stalks, and the mint leaves or Thai basil.
3. To make the dressing, deseed and finely chop the chilli. Grate the ginger, before squeezing out the juice. Discard the remains. Halve the lime and then squeeze out the juice. Mix everything together with the other ingredients for the dressing.
4. Mix the noodles, beansprouts and herbs.
5. Shred the salad into pieces and place on a large plate. Top with noodles, cucumber and mango. Pour the dressing over it. Sprinkle the chopped nuts and toasted coconut chips on top.

Salad with saffron potatoes, beans and eggs

Saffron is a spice for potatoes, particularly when the two are accompanied by an acidic chilli dressing. Pour the dressing onto the warm potatoes so that they absorb all the delicious flavours. If you are on the brink of ruin, you can use 1 teaspoon of turmeric instead of saffron. Smoked coconut chips provide a good smoky flavour and a little bit of crispiness, but it's also fine to use smoked almonds – bought or home-made.

1. Cook the lentils following the instructions on the pack.
2. Wash and cut the potatoes into smaller pieces. Cook them until soft in salted water for 15–20 minutes.
3. In the meantime, soft boil the eggs for 6–7 minutes. Rinse them to cool them, then peel them and halve them once cool.
4. To make the dressing, mix the saffron with the hot water in a bowl. Mix the saffron water with all the other ingredients for the dressing. Season with salt and pepper to taste.
5. Halve the haricots verts and put them in a bowl. Pour the potato water over the beans and leave them to stand for a minute while they soften.
6. Pour the dressing over the potatoes while they are still warm.
7. Plate the salad. Add the potatoes, lentils, haricots verts and tomatoes. Top with smoked coconut chips and the halved eggs.

SERVES 4

100 g (3½ oz/½ cup) uncooked green lentils

800 g (1 lb 12 oz) potatoes

4 eggs

150 g (5 oz) haricots verts

80 g (3 oz) small leaf salad, e.g. bistro mix

250 g (9 oz) cherry tomatoes, halved

100 g (3½ oz/2 cups) smoked coconut chips or smoked almonds (page 176)

SAFFRON DRESSING

a pinch of saffron

1 tablespoon hot water

1 red chilli, seeded and finely chopped

4 tablespoons olive oil

1 tablespoon white wine vinegar

2 teaspoons honey

zest and juice from ½ lemon

salt and freshly ground black pepper

VEGAN

Skip the eggs and use agave syrup instead of honey.

FILLED BREAD

Peel and coarsely grate the carrot. Mix the leftover salad with quark and mayonnaise to form a creamy mixture. Flavour with a little curry powder, sweet chilli sauce, salt and chilli flakes. Put the mixture into pitta breads or rolls.

Salad with roasted chickpeas, peaches and whisked lemon ricotta

A salad with crispy chickpeas (garbanzos), sweet peaches and salty cheese is the meal for you when you're after a light vegetable-based dish. I usually use seasonal fruits. Once the peaches are out of season, I prefer to use pears or melons. The chickpeas can be used not only for sprinkling on salads but also in stews or as snacks on their own. If you want them even crispier, mix the cornflour (cornstarch) with a little polenta (cornmeal) and finely grated Parmesan before putting them in the pan.

SERVES 4

3 ripe peaches

1 cucumber

1 lettuce

ROASTED CHICKPEAS

400 g (14 oz) tin chickpeas (garbanzos)

1 tablespoon cornflour (cornstarch)

1 teaspoon paprika

4 sprigs of rosemary or 40 sage leaves

olive oil, for frying

salt

LEMON RICOTTA

250 g (9 oz) ricotta

zest of 1 lemon

3 tablespoons yoghurt (optional)

2 teaspoons freshly squeezed lemon juice

LEMON DRESSING

3 tablespoons olive oil

1 tablespoon freshly squeezed lemon juice

1 tablespoon honey

chilli (hot pepper) flakes, salt and freshly ground black pepper

1. Drain the chickpeas. Rinse them and dry on a tea towel, trying to get them as dry as possible. Then put them in a bowl and mix with cornflour, paprika and herbs.
2. Heat up the oil in a large frying pan (skillet) and add the chickpeas. Lower the heat and fry them until crisp for 5–10 minutes. Stir occasionally. Take care, as it may spit if there is a lot of water left and the heat is high. Season with salt.
3. Whisk the ricotta and the lemon zest. Add yoghurt if you think the ricotta is dry and whisk for a little longer. Season with lemon juice.
4. Mix the ingredients for the dressing. Season with chilli flakes, salt and freshly ground black pepper to taste.
5. Cut the peaches into wedges. Peel and deseed the cucumber and cut into semi-circles. Cut the salad into pieces.
6. Spread the ricotta on plates. Add the salad, cucumber and peaches. Pour the dressing over it and top with chickpeas.

VEGAN

Use tofotta (page 42) instead of ricotta and swap honey for agave syrup.

GREEN SIDES

Pak choi with brown soy butter

With butter-fried vegetables like this on the table, there's a big risk or even likelihood that the side dish will run out first. If you like heat, why not add some grated ginger or finely chopped chilli.

SERVES 4–6

400 g (14 oz) pak choi (bok choi)

40 g (1½ oz) butter

1½ tablespoon Japanese soy sauce

1 red chilli, seeded and finely chopped

rapeseed (canola) oil, for frying

2 tablespoons furikake (page 179) or roasted sesame seeds

coriander (cilantro) leaves, to garnish

1. Split the pak choi lengthways.
2. Brown the butter in a saucepan or frying pan (skillet) until it smells nutty and is light brown in colour. Pour in the soy sauce and the chilli, and then pour the butter into a bowl to stop the browning process.
3. Fry the cut edge of the pak choi in oil for approximately 2 minutes until it has taken on colour and softened. Consider covering with a lid so that the pak choi is steamed.
4. Place onto a plate. Pour over the butter, top with furikake or roasted sesame seeds and use scissors to snip the coriander over it, including the stalks. Serve immediately.

Edamame beans with ginger dressing

Soybeans in their skins are known as edamame beans. You can find them in the supermarket freezer and in the space of just a few minutes they make one of the tastiest snacks ever – at least if being healthy is part of the equation. The beans shouldn't be peeled – just eat them straight out of the skin. Skip the dressing for an even healthier snack.

SERVES 4–6

300 g (10½ oz) frozen edamame beans

3 tablespoons furikake (page 179) or roasted sesame seeds

GINGER DRESSING

40 g (1½ oz) ginger

1 garlic clove, finely chopped

2 tablespoons rapeseed (canola) oil

1 tablespoon mirin or sugar

1 tablespoon Japanese soy sauce

2 teaspoons freshly squeezed lime juice

1 teaspoon sesame oil

1. Add water to the beans in a saucepan over a medium-low heat. Add salt.
2. Peel and finely grate the ginger. Squeeze the juice and discard the remains. Mix the juice with the garlic and all the other ingredients for the dressing.
3. Cook the beans until al dente. Drain the water and pour the dressing over them while they are still warm.
4. Top with furikake and salt, and serve immediately.

Hari fries with Parmesan

You can make delicious and crisp 'bean fries' by roasting green beans in the oven. It's vital that the beans are dry and the recipe only works with fresh beans. If you only have frozen beans, you can fry them in oil and garlic instead, and grate a little Parmesan and lemon zest on top when serving.

SERVES 4

150 g (5 oz) fresh haricots verts or wax beans

100 g (3½ oz/¾ cup) plain (all-purpose) flour, chickpea (gram) flour or cornflour (cornstarch)

3 eggs

250 g (8½ oz/4 cups) panko breadcrumbs

75 g (2½ oz) Parmesan, finely grated

zest of 1 lemon

1. Preheat the oven to 225°C (437°F/Gas 7).
2. Rinse the beans. Dry them using kitchen paper.
3. Put the flour in a deep dish or bowl. Whisk the eggs and pour them into a square tin or bowl. Crumble the panko breadcrumbs if they are large crumbs and mix in the cheese and lemon zest. Pour the mixture into a bowl, preferably a square one.
4. First turn the beans in the flour, then in the whisked egg, and finally in the panko breadcrumbs.
5. Lay out the beans one by one onto a tray lined with baking paper, put in the oven and roast for 15–20 minutes, turning halfway through cooking.

Pimientos de padrón with peanut sprinkles

Pimientos de padrón are small, mild green chillies, originally from Galicia in Spain. Shichimi togarashi is a Japanese chilli mixture that is delicious but difficult to pronounce. As luck would have it, you can just say shichimi, or you can use chilli flakes instead.

SERVES 4

salt

4 tablespoons salted peanuts

200 g (7 oz) pimientos de padrón

rapeseed (canola) oil, for frying

1 tablespoon sesame oil

shichimi togarashi or chilli flakes

1. Finely chop or blend the peanuts to form a fine consistency.
2. Fry the chillies in rapeseed oil in a large frying pan (skillet) until they soften and have taken on colour.
3. Serve topped with peanuts, sesame oil and shichimi togarashi or chilli flakes.

PAK CHOI WITH BROWN SOY BUTTER (PAGE 146)   •   EDAMAME BEANS WITH GINGER DRESSING (PAGE 146)

HARI FRIES WITH PARMESAN (PAGE 147) ● PIMIENTOS DE PADRÓN WITH PEANUT SPRINKLES (PAGE 147)

149

Broccoli with miso dressing

Miso is one of my favourite flavourings in tomato sauces, but also for dressings too. This version is reminiscent of a vinaigrette, which is great not just with broccoli but also with raw grated carrots or shredded iceberg lettuce.

SERVES 4–6

500 g (1 lb 2 oz) broccoli

3 tablespoons sesame seeds

3 tablespoons crispy onions

coriander (cilantro)
leaves, to garnish

MISO DRESSING

30 g (1 oz) ginger

2 tablespoons white miso

3 tablespoons mirin
or agave syrup

1 tablespoon rice vinegar

1 teaspoon light soy sauce

4 tablespoons mild olive oil

salt

1. Boil water for the broccoli. Add salt.
2. To make the dressing, peel and finely grate the ginger. Squeeze the juice and discard the remains. Mix the juice with all the ingredients for the dressing, apart from the oil and salt, in a bowl. Slowly add the oil while whisking. If necessary, add cold water to achieve the right consistency. Season with salt.
3. Break the broccoli into florets, remove the stalks and cut into smaller pieces. Cook the broccoli in the boiling water until al dente.
4. Toast the sesame seeds in a dry frying pan (skillet) without any fat. Mix with the crispy onions.
5. Pour the dressing over the broccoli and top with the seed and onion mixture. Garnish with coriander leaves.

Broccoli and asparagus with miso butter

A deluxe vegetable dish that works well as a starter or side. Add soft boiled or poached eggs if you want to serve it as a starter. The butter also tastes great with oven-roasted celeriac or cooked Jerusalem artichokes.

SERVES 4–6

250 g (9 oz) asparagus

250 g (9 oz) broccoli

1 red chilli, seeded and
finely chopped

50 g (2 oz) spring onions
(scallions), shredded

olive oil, for frying

MISO BUTTER

50 g (2 oz) butter at
room temperature

2 teaspoons white miso

1. Boil water for the vegetables. Add salt.
2. Mix the butter with the miso.
3. Cut away the harder, lower part of the asparagus. Cut off the broccoli florets and cut the stalk into smaller pieces.
4. Cook the broccoli in the boiling water until al dente. Then, fry the asparagus and broccoli in olive oil for a few minutes until tender and slightly browned. Mix with the butter and top with chilli and spring onions.

Green peas and beans with mint and lemon dressing

Fresh peas and beans are naturally delicious, but it's always good to have frozen ones on hand. If you eat cheese, why not grate a little Parmesan or pecorino on top? If you don't have any mint leaves, you can skip this or use basil instead.

SERVES 4–6

200 g (7 oz) green peas, preferably petits pois

150 g (5 oz) haricots verts, frozen or fresh

150 g (5 oz) wax beans, frozen or fresh

4 tablespoons hazelnuts

MINT AND LEMON DRESSING

3 tablespoons olive oil

1 tablespoon white balsamic vinegar

zest and juice of 1 lemon

1 teaspoon agave syrup

big bunch of mint leaves

salt and freshly ground black pepper

1. Boil water for the peas and broccoli. Add salt.
2. Mix all the ingredients for the dressing, apart from the mint. Finely chop half of the mint leaves and mix them in. Save the rest to garnish. Season with salt and pepper to taste.
3. Cook the peas and beans until al dente.
4. Toast the nuts in a dry frying pan (skillet) and roughly chop them once they have cooled.
5. Pour the dressing over the peas and beans and top with the rest of the mint leaves and the nuts.

Lemon-marinated red onion

A speedy condiment to make that is great with favourites like hamburgers and tacos, but also goes well on a lentil salad. The onions are nicest when eaten immediately.

SERVES 4

2 red onions

1 lemon

2 teaspoons agave syrup

salt

1. Peel and thinly slice the red onions, and place them in a bowl.
2. Squeeze and zest the lemon. Mix into a marinade together with the agave syrup and a pinch of salt.
3. Pour the marinade over the onions and massage for a minute or so.

SERVES 4

100 g (3½ oz) mixed greens,
e.g. salad leaves, pea sprouts,
sunflower sprouts, kale

toasted nuts or seeds

DRESSING

2 avocados

big bunch of basil leaves

big bunch of flat-leaf parsley

1 teaspoon tarragon
leaves, fresh or dried

1 garlic clove, sliced

2 tablespoons
nutritional yeast

2 tablespoons white
balsamic vinegar

3 tablespoons olive oil

2 tablespoons cold water

salt and cayenne pepper

Green salad and green goddess dressing with avocado

The original recipe for this green goddess dressing contains mayonnaise and anchovies. This is a vegan version made using avocado, which is just as divinely delicious. Different toasted seeds or croutons work well with it.

1. Remove the stones from the avocados and blitz the avocado flesh and herbs using a hand-held blender or food processor.
2. Peel and slice the bok choi. Add with nutritional yeast and vinegar and mix a little more.
3. Add the oil a little at a time while mixing, then add water to achieve desired consistency. Season with salt and cayenne pepper to taste.
4. Mix the salad with the other greens and drizzle the dressing onto it. Top with toasted nuts or seeds.

SERVES 4

300 g (10½ oz) Brussels sprouts

1–2 avocados

3 tablespoons dukkah
(page 178)

3 tablespoons olive oil

1½ tablespoons freshly
squeezed lemon juice

Avocado and Brussels sprout salad with dukkah

Boiled Brussels sprouts aren't one of my favourite things, but I think they're delicious when raw or roasted. In this salad, they're thinly sliced and in good company with grilled avocado that provides creaminess and some smokiness. The dukkah provides flavour, salt and crispiness.

1. Remove the hard cores, then thinly slice the Brussels sprouts .
2. Remove the stone from the avocados, peel and slice the flesh into wedges. Grill them in a grill pan until they are stripy. Cut them into smaller pieces. Plate up the Brussels sprouts, avocado and dukkah.
3. Mix the oil and lemon juice and pour over.

GREEN PEAS AND BEANS WITH MINT AND LEMON DRESSING (PAGE 152) • **LEMON-MARINATED RED ONION (PAGE 152)**

GREEN SALAD AND GREEN GODDESS DRESSING WITH AVOCADO (PAGE 153) • AVOCADO AND BRUSSELS SPROUT SALAD WITH DUKKAH (PAGE 153)

Mashed beans with dill

I've swapped the cucumber in the classic Greek tzatziki for beans that I mash. Sometimes I don't even mash them but mix in a little cucumber, making it more like the original. Great with halloumi and tomato and potato dishes.

1. Save a few sprigs of dill to garnish and finely chop the rest. Drain the beans.
2. Mix the garlic, dill and beans with vinegar and yoghurt. Lightly mash the beans and add salt and freshly ground black pepper.

SERVES 4

big bunch of dill

400 g (14 oz) tin butter
(lima) beans

1 garlic clove, finely chopped

1 teaspoon red wine vinegar

300 g (10½ oz/1¼ cups)
Turkish yoghurt

salt and freshly ground
black pepper

SERVES 4

300 g (10½ oz) red cabbage

100 g (3½ oz) kale

big bunch of coriander
(cilantro) leaves

1 orange

3 tablespoons salad seed
sprinkles (page 178) or
other toasted nuts

TAHINI DRESSING WITH CHILLI

4 tablespoons tahini

2 teaspoons apple
cider vinegar

1 teaspoon maple syrup

1–2 teaspoon harissa
or sriracha

60 ml (2 fl oz/¼ cup) cold water

salt and freshly ground
black pepper

Red cabbage and orange salad with tahini dressing

If you're afraid of overdosing on cabbage, you can make the salad using carrots instead. Harissa is a hot and tasty North African spice paste with chilli. The tahini dressing lasts for up to a week in the fridge and goes well with most vegetables, as well as being delicious when drizzled on freshly baked pizza or with falafels.

1. Finely shred the red cabbage and tear the kale into pieces. Chop the coriander up finely, including the stalks, and peel and cut the orange into wedges. Mix everything on one plate.
2. Whisk together all the dressing ingredients and dilute with cold water to achieve the desired consistency. Season with salt and freshly ground black pepper and pour the dressing over the cabbage and orange wedges. Top with salad seed sprinkles.

200 g (7 oz) fennel

150 g (5 oz) cabbage

1 apple

3 tablespoons nuts or
seeds, e.g. toasted pumpkin
seeds, melon seeds or
smoked almonds

MUSTARD DRESSING

1 tablespoon cold-pressed,
nutty rapeseed
(canola) or olive oil

2 tablespoons neutral
rapeseed (canola) oil

1 tablespoon white
balsamic vinegar

1 teaspoon Dijon mustard

salt and freshly ground
black pepper

SERVES 4

250 g (9 oz) frozen
soybeans, defrosted

1–2 avocados

1 garlic clove, finely chopped

1–2 tablespoons white miso

zest and juice of 1 lime

salt and cayenne pepper

Fennel salad with white cabbage, apple and mustard dressing

Pizza salad 2.0. The cold-pressed rapeseed (canola) oil has a good, nutty flavour, but you can also use something like olive oil. Consider sprinkling some pomegranate seeds on top if you want a little extra colour.

1. Mix all the ingredients for the dressing. Season with salt and pepper to taste.
2. Finely shred the fennel, white cabbage and apple and mix with the dressing.
3. Roughly chop the nuts or seeds (or both) and sprinkle on top.

Soybeans with avocado and lime

Japan meets Mexico. Sweet green beans make for a good-looking and well-balanced dish if you mix them with lime, avocado and miso. They are not only healthy but also tasty in a sandwich or alongside a Mexican-inspired dish.

1. Remove the stone from the avocados.
2. Mix the soybeans with the avocado flesh, garlic, miso and lime juice.
3. Add the lime zest and season with salt and a little cayenne pepper. Dilute with water if you want a less firm consistency.

MASHED BEANS WITH DILL (PAGE 156) • **RED CABBAGE AND ORANGE SALAD WITH TAHINI DRESSING (PAGE 156)**

FENNEL SALAD WITH WHITE CABBAGE, APPLE AND MUSTARD DRESSING (PAGE 157) • SOYBEANS WITH AVOCADO AND LIME (PAGE 157)

Kohlrabi with soy sauce and lime dressing

A simple soy sauce dressing works well with any vegetable, but why not use the underestimated kohlrabi? It's incredibly crispy and tastes great with sweet pears, toasted seeds and some salty dressing.

SERVES 4

3 tablespoons sesame seeds

1 kohlrabi, finely sliced

1 pear, sliced

70 g (2¼ oz) small leaf salad

DRESSING

3 tablespoons olive oil

1 tablespoon Japanese soy sauce

1 tablespoon freshly squeezed lime juice

1 teaspoon agave syrup

1. Mix all the ingredients for the dressing.
2. Toast the sesame seeds in a dry frying pan (skillet).
3. Mix the kohlrabi and pear slices with the salad on a plate, pour over the dressing and top with sesame seeds.

Lentil mash with miso

Tinned red lentils are available, but they're not as tasty – so I recommend you cook your own. You can follow the instructions on the pack and cook the lentils until completely soft, although I think it's better if you cook them until al dente. The mash is good for dipping vegetables in, putting in a sandwich or dolloping on top of a salad.

SERVES 4

150 g (5 oz/¾ cup) dried red lentils

1 tablespoon white miso

½ teaspoon ground coriander

½ teaspoon ground ginger

pinch of chilli flakes

1 tablespoon olive oil and chopped flat-leaf parsley, to serve

1. Cook the lentils, preferably until al dente. Drain and leave to cool.
2. Mix the lentils with the miso, coriander, ginger and chilli flakes to form a mash.
3. Pour into a bowl and top with olive oil. Sprinkle a little chopped flat-leaf parsley on top.

GREEN IS GOOD

2 carrots

2 beetroots (beets),
e.g. polka or yellow

100 g (3½ oz) pea shoots

50 g (2 oz/⅓ cup) salted
cashews, chopped

DRESSING

2 passion fruits

1 red chilli, seeded and
finely chopped

3 tablespoons mild olive oil

1 tablespoon white
balsamic vinegar

1 teaspoon agave syrup

salt

SERVES 4

400 g (14 oz) tin
cannellini beans

250 g (9 oz) artichokes in oil

1 garlic clove, finely chopped

3 tablespoons
nutritional yeast

oil from the artichokes
or truffle oil

zest of 1 lemon

salt and freshly ground
black pepper

Colourful salad with passion fruit dressing

A vibrantly colourful salad on the dinner table is usually impossible to resist eating, especially when it contains passion fruit and salted nuts. If you want even more colour in your salad, you could shred a little red cabbage or unripened mango into it.

1. Halve the passion fruits and scoop out the flesh. Mix the flesh with the other ingredients for the dressing. Season with salt.
2. Peel the carrots and beetroots. Finely grate or slice them with a mandolin.
3. Mix the carrots, beetroots and pea shoots with the dressing on a plate or in a bowl.
4. Sprinkle the nuts over the salad.

Artichokes with cannellini beans

Preparing artichokes is time-consuming so a jar is the ideal situation. Good with pasta dishes and in salads or sandwiches, preferably grilled.

1. Drain the beans. Remove the artichokes from the oil.
2. Put the beans, artichoke, garlic and yeast into a food processor and blend into a mash.
3. Dilute with oil to the desired consistency and season with lemon zest, salt and pepper.

COLOURFUL SALAD WITH PASSION FRUIT DRESSING (PAGE 161)   •   ARTICHOKE WITH CANNELLINI BEANS (PAGE 161)

Carrot hummus with peanut butter

This hummus gains a little extra colour, flavour and vitamins from carrots. If you don't have a food processor, you may want to cook the carrots until soft before mixing them. Vary the recipe by mixing in spices like caraway, coriander and paprika that you have toasted in a frying pan (skillet).

SERVES 4

1 large carrot

3 garlic cloves, peeled

400 g (14 oz) tin chickpeas (garbanzos)

2 tablespoons peanut butter

1 tablespoon freshly squeezed lemon juice

1 teaspoon ground cumin

1–2 teaspoons sriracha

salt

1. Peel the carrot and cut it into thin slices. Boil the carrot slices and garlic for around 5 minutes in salted water until soft.
2. Drain the chickpeas and put into a food processor with the carrots and garlic. Add the peanut butter, lemon juice and cumin, and mix until it is a smooth hummus.
3. Season with sriracha and salt to taste.

Mashed avocado with beans and tahini

Tahini is a cream made with toasted sesame seeds. I prefer the lighter oriental version that is made using peeled seeds. This is amazing on toasted sourdough, with eggs and salads.

SERVES 4

400 g (14 oz) tin chickpeas (garbanzos)

2 avocados

1 garlic clove, peeled

1 teaspoon ground cumin

1 tablespoon freshly squeezed lemon juice

2 tablespoons tahini

1 green chilli, seeded and finely chopped

small bunch of coriander (cilantro) leaves

salt and olive oil, to finish

1. Drain the chickpeas.
2. Remove the stones from the avocados.
3. Blend the chickpeas, avocado flesh and garlic with cumin, lemon juice and tahini for a couple of minutes in a food processor.
4. Chop the coriander, including the stalks. Mix the coriander and chilli into the chickpea mixture and season with salt. Drizzle a little olive oil on top. Garnish with coriander.

Mashed black beans with tomatoes and chipotle

SERVES 4

400 g (14 oz) tin black beans

1 tablespoon chipotle paste

1 teaspoon cocoa powder

1 tablespoon freshly
squeezed lime juice

½ bunch of coriander

2 tablespoons sundried
tomatoes, shredded

salt and freshly ground pepper

It might not be the best looking mash, but it's delicious if you love coriander and smoky chilli. Naturally, it's great on tortilla wraps and with Mexican food, but you can also have it on bread, with roasted carrots or to dunk vegetables into.

1. Drain the beans.
2. Mix the beans, chipotle, cocoa and lime juice into a mash using a mixer or food processor. Chop the coriander, including the stalks.
3. Stir in the sundried tomatoes and add salt and pepper to taste. Dilute with water if you want a less firm mash.

Grilled pepper hummus with walnuts

SERVES 4

50 g (2 oz) walnuts

400 g (14 oz) tin chickpeas
(garbanzos)

200 g (7 oz) tin grilled peppers

2 tablespoons tahini

1 tablespoon freshly
squeezed lemon juice

1 teaspoon ground cumin

salt and freshly ground
black pepper

When peppers are in season, you can grill fresh ones. The rest of the year it's fine to use peppers from a tin or jar. This hummus mixture is great with all sorts of Mediterranean dishes and for dipping vegetables into.

1. Toast the walnuts in a frying pan without any fat.
2. Drain the chickpeas. Drain the peppers.
3. Mix all the ingredients using a blender or food processor. Add water to achieve the desired consistency. Season with salt and pepper to taste.

MASHED BLACK BEANS WITH TOMATOES AND CHIPOTLE (PAGE 165) • **GRILLED PEPPER HUMMUS WITH WALNUTS (PAGE 165)**

BASIC RECIPES

Some ingredients, like cooked beans and vegesan, appear frequently in the book. You can buy most things ready-made in the shops, but it tastes better and is cheaper if you make it yourself. If you can, keep some of these things in the freezer, fridge or larder to speed up cooking when hunger is knocking on the door.

COOKED BEANS

Beans, lentils and peas are the vegetable lover's best friend when it comes to protein. King among these is the soybean, which has the highest protein content of any vegetable. There are lots of types.

Many people think you have to soak beans before cooking them. You don't, but there are advantages to doing so. One is that the cooking time is halved, while another is that the risk of flatulence and unwelcome odour experiences is minimised. Beans contain lectins, a substance that the body struggles to break down but which disappears when soaked and cooked. The quantity of lectins varies depending on the bean, and in its wisdom nature has given us stomachs that vary in terms of their sensitivity to the substance. I was given a forgiving stomach, but a rather forgetful brain – so I usually skip soaking. I boil beans in water and let them cook for about 15 minutes. Then I drain the water, fill up with fresh water and simmer the beans for a long time over a medium-low heat. The cooking time varies depending on type, but just as with all other cookery, there's a good way to find out when the food is ready: taste it!

Think freely when it comes to flavouring. Onions are always good to have, and vinegar-cooked beans are delicious in salads. Bay leaves can be swapped for thyme or oregano. Smoked paprika or smoked oil provides a really smoky flavour and ginger and chilli provide heat.

One of the best bean tips is to cook a big batch. Cook the beans until al dente, then allow them to cool in the cooking water so that they absorb all the delicious flavours. You can freeze the beans in appropriately sized containers. A tetrapak or tin from the supermarket often weighs 400 g (14 oz). This is the equivalent of 300 g (10½ oz/1½ cups) of cooked beans.

WITH SOAKING, MAKES 1½–2 KG (3 LB 3 OZ–4 LB 4 OZ)

500 g (1 lb 2 oz/2½ cups) dried beans

2 yellow onions

5 garlic cloves, peeled

3 sprigs of rosemary

1 bay leaf

salt

1. Soak the beans for 18–24 hours. The longer they are soaked, the less time they need to be cooked. Drain the water.
2. Peel and chop the onions into wedges. Boil the onions, garlic, herbs, salt and beans in approximately 4 litres (8½ pints/16 cups) of water over a medium heat until the beans are soft but still have a core, for approximately 45 minutes. Cooking time varies depending on how long the beans have been soaked for, which type of beans are being used, and whether the beans are new or old. Add more water if it boils off.
3. Leave the beans to cool in the cooking water. If the beans are still too hard when they have cooled, you can put the saucepan on the hob and boil them again until you achieve the desired consistency. Keep in the fridge for up to 6 days or freeze.

WITHOUT SOAKING

1. Put the beans in a saucepan and fill with approximately 1 litre (34 fl oz/4 cups) of water. Bring to boil and simmer for about 15 minutes.
2. Drain the water and fill with approximately 4 litres (140 fl oz/16 cups) of new water. Add salt.
3. Cook according to the instructions for soaked beans. Cooking time is 1½–2½ hours.

COOKED LENTILS

Lentils come in many different colours – red, green, yellow, brown and black. Some unknown individual decided that the black ones were best and christened them beluga lentils because the uncooked lentils look like the caviar of the same name. Cooking time varies quite a lot depending on type, but no lentil needs to be soaked or cooked for more than 35 minutes.

Just as with beans, you may want to flavour the cooking water. This is especially effective with green and black lentils, which have a slightly longer cooking time. Onions and vinegar are good flavours if the lentils are for a salad. There are generally good instructions on the packaging and you can always add a little extra seasoning.

Feel free to skip the cooking instructions on red lentil packaging. Most tell you to cook the lentils for 10 minutes. This is fine if you enjoy eating a red sludge. If you follow the below recipe, you will be rewarded with nutty lentils with a little bit of bite.

Lentils can be frozen, although they turn a little mushy after being defrosted, which makes them best suited to patties or stews.

RED LENTILS, MAKES 300 G (3½ OZ/1¼ CUPS)

500 ml (17 fl oz/2 cups) water

100 g (3½ oz/⅓ cup) dried red lentils

salt

1. Bring a pan of salted water to the boil, or fill from the kettle. Add the lentils, stir them and cook for exactly 2 minutes under a lid.
2. Remove from the heat, stir and leave with the lid on for around 2 minutes. Stir and taste them. If they are suitably al dente, you can drain the water. Otherwise leave them to stand for another minute or so.

VINEGAR-COOKED GREEN OR BLACK LENTILS, MAKES APPROXIMATELY 300 G (3½ OZ/1⅓ CUPS)

600 ml (20 fl oz/2½ cups) water

1 large yellow onion, peeled

2 garlic cloves, peeled

2 sprigs of rosemary

1 tablespoon red wine vinegar

100 g (3½ oz/½ cup) dried green or black lentils

salt

1. Bring a pan of salted water to the boil, or fill from the kettle. Halve the onion and place it into the boiling water in a pan together with the garlic, rosemary, vinegar and lentils. Cook for 20–35 minutes until the lentils are al dente. Adjust the cooking time based on the lentil type.
2. Remove from the heat and leave to cool in the pan. Stir occasionally. Pour into a bowl or onto a plate if you want it to cool quicker and to stop the cooking process.
3. Drain the water.

SPROUTS AND SHOOTS

Sprouting lentils, beans or seeds is good in a number of ways. In part, the nutritional content actually increases, while our bodies are also more easily able to absorb the nutrients.

Sprouts and shoots are perfect to use when winter has put its mark on the ground and imported vegetables are tasteless and expensive. It's also easy to sprout, but you must have a certain degree of patience.

Among the easiest to sprout are mung beans, red lentils, buckwheat, white quinoa and alfalfa seeds.

Shoots are most easily achieved with seeds from cress, radish and mustard. It also works well to put shoots on sunflower seeds, but you need to use the ones with shells that are normally fed to birds. Yellow peas also work, but must be activated – sprouted – beforehand, which means they take a little longer.

TO SPROUT YOU NEED:

glass jar, sieve, gauze and rubber band or sprouting jar

paper bag or larder where the jar can be left in the dark

seeds, beans or lentils (see above)

1. Rinse what you are going to sprout in cold water. Then soak it in a bowl with lukewarm water for 8 hours. Drain the water and rinse a couple of times.
2. Put the seeds, beans or lentils in a glass jar, sprouting jar or a colander. Put a gauze on the jar, or put on the lid of the sprouting jar or a moist tea towel over the colander.
3. Put the jar on a tray in a dark room at room temperature or in a larder. A moist tea towel works well, or you can use a paper bag. The sprouts should be kept moist but not wet, and should be rinsed 2–3 times per day. After 3–6 days, the sprouts will be fully grown.
4. You can now put the jar in sunlight. This will make the sprouts greener and healthier.

TO GET SHOOTS YOU NEED:

kitchen paper

smaller seeds, e.g. from cress, radish, mustard, broccoli

1. Put the seeds on a moistened piece of kitchen paper. Cover with cling film (plastic wrap), ensuring that it is not sealed completely, and leave in the light at room temperature. Keep the paper moist, for example by using a water spray gun.
2. Remove the cling film (plastic wrap) after a few days when shoots begin to show. Continue to keep the seeds moist. The shoots will be ready after around a week.

KIMCHI

This Korean fermented cabbage dish is spicy and slightly addictive. It normally contains fish sauce, but this is a vegan version made with miso instead. Once you've got started with the fermentation, you can add other vegetables or fruit, such as grated radish, rhubarb, mango or yellow onion. The kimchi will keep for several months if you don't put any naughty fingers or dirty spoons inside the jar. Korean chilli peppers are available in Asian stores.

MAKES APPROXIMATELY 1 KG (2 LB 3 OZ)

1 kg (2 lb 3 oz) Chinese cabbage, preferably organic

2 tablespoons sugar

1 tablespoon iodine-free salt

4 garlic cloves, peeled and grated

60 g (2 oz) ginger

2 tablespoons white miso

2–4 tablespoons gochugaru (Korean chilli pepper)

100 g (3½ oz) spring onions (scallions), shredded

1 carrot, peeled and grated

1. Cut up and shred the cabbage. Layer the cabbage, half the sugar and salt in a bowl. Put in the fridge for around 24 hours.
2. Rinse the cabbage and leave to dry in a colander.
3. Peel and finely grate the ginger, before squeezing out the juice. Mix the garlic and ginger juice with the remaining sugar, miso and gochugaru into a paste in a large bowl. Mix in the spring onions, carrot and cabbage.
4. Massage in the paste using your hands – preferably without gloves. This is because your hands have healthy bacteria that help to start to the fermentation process. Massage until liquid is squeezed from the cabbage.
5. Fill a glass jar with a snap-on lid with cabbage. Press down the cabbage so that it is completely covered with liquid and then put on the lid. If it isn't covered, you may need to add a little boiling water and stir it. The jar should not be filled to the top – make sure there is a 3 cm (1 in) gap at the top. Put the jar on a plate by a window so that the fermentation gets started quicker.
6. After 3–5 days, the cabbage should start to bubble and smell a little acidic. It is now ready to eat. Put the jar in the fridge and allow the flavours to mature so that the kimchi is even tastier.

QUICK SAUERKRAUT KIMCHI

Sometimes, when I don't have any kimchi in, I make a speedy cheat's version that is just as healthy since it's based on sauerkraut. Of course, it doesn't taste the same, but it's good on its own terms.

MAKES APPROXIMATELY 500 G (1 LB 2 OZ)

40 g (1½ oz) ginger

1 garlic clove, finely grated

1 tablespoon gochugaru (Korean chilli pepper) or 1 teaspoon sambal oelek, plus 1 teaspoon chilli flakes

2 tablespoons chilli sauce

1 carrot, peeled and coarsely grated

400 g (14 oz) sauerkraut

1. Peel and finely grate the ginger, before squeezing out the juice. Mix the garlic and ginger juice with the gochugaru and chilli sauce to form a red paste.
2. Mix with the sauerkraut and carrot.

EGG–FREE MAYONNAISE

Vegan mayonnaise without eggs, also known as vega-naise, is easy to make at home. Here are two great recipes that can be made using a hand-held blender and a high-sided mixing bowl. They are both surpris-ingly similar to ordinary mayonnaise. Flavour them with things like curry powder and mango chutney, sriracha and finely zested lime, Japanese soy sauce and finely grated ginger or white miso.

WITH CHICKPEA AQUAFABA, MAKES APPROXIMATELY 300 G (10½ OZ/1¼ CUPS)

2 tablespoons tinned chickpeas (garbanzos)

2 teaspoons Dijon mustard

3 tablespoons aquafaba

250 ml (8½ fl oz/1 cup) rapeseed (canola) oil

1 teaspoon freshly squeezed lemon juice

salt

1. Ensure that all the ingredients are at room temperature. Put the chickpeas, mustard and aquafaba in a high-sided mixing bowl (to use a hand-held blender) or a food processor.
2. Mix everything together thoroughly. Add the oil a little at a time and mix until the mayonnaise is combined and has the desired consistency. Season with lemon juice and salt to taste. The mayonnaise will keep for around 5 days in the fridge.

WITH SOY MILK, MAKES APPROXIMATELY 300 G (10½ OZ/1¼ CUPS)

150 ml (5 fl oz/⅔ cup) unsweetened soy milk

2 teaspoons Dijon mustard

1 teaspoon white wine vinegar

250 ml (8½ fl oz/1 cup) rapeseed (canola) oil

1 teaspoon freshly squeezed lemon juice

salt

1. Ensure that all the ingredients are at room temperature. Put the soy milk, mustard and vinegar in a high-sided mixing bowl (to use a hand-held blender) or a food processor.
2. Mix everything together thoroughly. Add the oil a little at a time and mix until the mayonnaise is combined and has the desired consistency. Season with lemon juice and salt to taste. The mayonnaise will keep for around 5 days in the fridge.

PANEER

To make this Indian fresh cheese without rennet, it's best to use a milk with as high a fat content as possible to ensure the cheese is creamy. The leftover whey is full of nutritional goodness. It's great for smoothies, baking, cooking rice and as a substitute for stock.

MAKES 400 G (14 OZ)

2 litres (70 fl oz/8 cups) high-fat milk

200 g (7 oz/1 cup) yoghurt

juice of 1 lemon

1½ teaspoons salt

1. Heat the milk and yoghurt in a heavy saucepan over a low heat. Whisk it occasionally to ensure the milk doesn't burn.
2. Take the saucepan off the heat when it begins to bubble and add the lemon juice and salt. Stir carefully with a spatula so that the milk divides into small cheese curds and a clear liquid forms. Leave to stand for around 5 minutes but stir carefully a couple of times until the cheese mass forms.
3. Pour it all through a straining cloth, or a coffee filter, and let all the whey run through. You can also catch the cheese mass with a slotted spoon and then place it on a straining cloth. Squeeze out the remaining whey by spinning the straining cloth like a ball.
4. Tip the cheese mass onto cling film (plastic wrap) and then transfer into a small mould. Apply a press. Place in the fridge for at least 2 hours, preferably 12.
5. Cut the cheese into pieces. It will keep for around 10 days in the fridge if it is well wrapped. You can freeze any leftover cheese.

FALAFEL

It's easy to make your own crispy falafels, but don't forget to soak the chickpeas (garbanzos) in advance. Make a double batch and freeze unfried balls. That's how they come from the supermarket freezer, but these ones are far tastier. Why not add chopped herbs for more flavour?

MAKES APPROXIMATELY 40 BALLS

250 g (9 oz/1 cup) dried chickpeas (garbanzos)

3 garlic cloves, finely chopped

1 tablespoon ground cumin

2 teaspoons ground coriander

pinch of cayenne pepper

1 teaspoon salt

1 tablespoon sesame oil

60 ml (2 fl oz/¼ cup) water

4 tablespoons cornflour (cornstarch)

100 g (3½ oz/⅔ cup) sesame seeds

neutral oil, for frying/deep-frying

1. Soak the chickpeas in cold water for 8–15 hours. Massage away some of the outer layers (it doesn't matter if some are left). Remove any black chickpeas. Drain the water.
2. Mix the garlic, chickpeas, spices, salt and sesame oil. Add the water, a little at a time, and mix into a batter. Add the cornflour until the batter is able to form balls that stick together. Add more water if the batter is too firm or more cornflour if it is too loose.
3. Pour out half of the sesame seeds onto baking paper. Spread out the batter on top and sprinkle with the rest of the sesame seeds. Form the batter into balls by hand.
4. Heat the oil in a frying pan (skillet) and fry or deep fry the balls in batches, for around 4 minutes per batch.

SMOKED ALMONDS AND COCONUTS

If you want to taste smoke without eating meat, you can flavour coconut and nuts with liquid smoke, smoked paprika, smoked chilli, smoked salt or smoked oil. You can also pour a little soy sauce in a hot frying pan so that it burns. Smoked almonds are available to buy in the shops. They are often sold under different names – smoked almonds, barbecued almonds or tamari roasted almonds .

SMOKED SOY ALMONDS, MAKES APPROXIMATELY 200 G (7 OZ/⅔ CUPS)

These almonds gain their smoky flavour from burnt soy sauce and smoked oil or smoked salt.

200 g (7 oz/⅔ cup) blanched almonds
2 tablespoons Japanese soy sauce
smoked oil or smoked rock salt

1. Toast the almonds in a frying pan (skillet) without any fat.
2. Pour the soy sauce over the almonds and leave to soak for a minute or so. Pour the smoked oil or smoked rock salt on top.
3. Leave to cool and store in an airtight container.

SMOKED ALMONDS WITH CHILLI, MAKES APPROXIMATELY 200 G (7 OZ/⅔ CUPS)

These almonds have a little heat and a smokier hickory flavour compared with the soy almonds.

4 tablespoons sugar
1 tablespoon liquid smoke
1 tablespoon chipotle paste
2 teaspoons salt
2 sprigs of rosemary
200 g (7 oz/⅔ cup) blanched almonds
rock salt or smoked rock salt

1. Set the oven to 200°C (400°F/Gas 6).
2. Boil all ingredients, except for the almonds and rock salt, in a saucepan. Add the almonds and leave to simmer for approximately 5 minutes over a medium heat.
3. Drain the liquid and place the almonds on a tray lined with baking paper. Roast for around 10 minutes until they take on some colour. Sprinkle with rock salt.
4. Leave to cool and store in an airtight container.

SMOKED COCONUT CHIPS, MAKES APPROXIMATELY 150 G (5 OZ/3 CUPS)

These chips are similar to bacon, even if they are a little sweeter. Great on pasta dishes and salads.

150 g (5 oz/3 cups) unroasted coconut chips
2 tablespoons rapeseed (canola) oil
1½ tablespoons Japanese soy sauce
1 tablespoon maple syrup
1½ teaspoons smoked paprika
1 teaspoon liquid smoke salt

1. Preheat the oven to 180°C (350°F/Gas 4).
2. Put the coconut in a bowl. Mix the oil, soy sauce, syrup, paprika and liquid smoke salt and pour on top. Season with salt.
3. Spread the chips in a baking pan lined baking paper and roast for around 5 minutes. Shake a few times while roasting and keep a close eye on them as they burn easily.
4. Allow to cool. Store in an airtight container.

QUICK PIZZA DOUGH

A quick dough that contains baking powder instead of yeast, which means it requires no time to prove. However, it does need to be thoroughly kneaded and it makes for slightly thicker pizzas. A good alternative to ready-made pizza bases and doughs available from the supermarket.

MAKES APPROXIMATELY 400 G (14 OZ) DOUGH, SERVES 2–3

210 g (7½ oz/1¾ cups) plain (all-purpose) flour

1½ teaspoons baking powder

½ teaspoon salt

200 g (7 oz/1 cup) yoghurt

1. Mix 180 g (6½ oz/1½ cups) of the flour, the baking powder and salt in a bowl. Add the yoghurt and work together into a dough.
2. Tip the dough onto a breadboard and knead for 5–10 minutes. Add flour, a little at a time, so that the dough doesn't stick. Work the dough until it feels smooth and isn't sticky.
3. Roll the dough into one large or two smaller pizza bases.

PIZZA DOUGH PROVED OVERNIGHT

If you're dreaming of thin and crispy pizzas, it's best to use cold-proved dough. Make a large batch and put proved balls in the freezer. You can also roll the balls out after proving and freeze them as ready-made pizza bases.

MAKES APPROXIMATELY 700 G (1 LB 9 OZ) DOUGH, SERVES 4–6

8 g (¼ oz) yeast

300 ml (10 fl oz/1¼ cups) cold water

2 teaspoons honey

3 tablespoons olive oil, plus extra for brushing

1½ teaspoons salt

540 g (1 lb 3½ oz/4⅓ cups) strong flour or another flour with high gluten content

1. Crumble the yeast in a bowl and add the water, honey and oil. Stir until the yeast has dissolved.
2. Add the salt and flour, a little at a time, and work together into a smooth and fairly loose dough. Work it for around 10 minutes by machine or 20 minutes by hand.
3. Form the dough into four or six round buns and place them in a roasting pan lined with cling film (plastic wrap). They will expand quite a lot, so don't put them too close together. Brush with olive oil and cover with cling film. Leave to prove for 12–24 hours in the fridge.
4. Roll out or stretch the dough into pizza bases.

PANKO AND LEMON SPRINKLES

Not unlike the Italian sprinkles known as gremolata, this version also contains crispy breadcrumbs and healthy nutritional yeast. Make a large batch and then freeze it. Then you can toast it straight from the freezer in a frying pan (skillet) for that newly fried feel. An extra teaspoon of chilli flakes will give an extra kick.

**MAKES APPROXIMATELY 200 G
(7 OZ/2–3 CUPS)**

1 garlic clove, finely chopped

200 g (7 oz/3⅓ cups) panko breadcrumbs or dry bread cut into small cubes

oil or butter, for frying

zest of 2 lemons

2 tablespoons nutritional yeast

100 g (3½ oz) finely chopped herbs

1. Fry the panko breadcrumbs or cubes of bread in oil or butter together with the garlic for a few minutes until they change colour.
2. Mix in the lemon zest, nutritional yeast and chopped herbs.

SALAD SEED SPRINKLES

Nut sprinkles are great for adding to salads, sliced avocado and pasta dishes, to name but a few. The seed mix keeps for a few weeks in an airtight container or for longer if you freeze it. You can also mix in a little chilli, shredded nori sheets, ground ginger or lime zest for added flavour.

**MAKES APPROXIMATELY 400 G
(14 OZ/3 CUPS)**

100 g (3½ oz/¾ cup) pumpkin seeds

100 g (3½ oz/¾ cup) flaxseeds

100 g (3½ oz/¾ cup) sunflower seeds

100 g (3½ oz/⅔ cup) sesame seeds

2 tablespoons nutritional yeast

1 teaspoon rock salt

1. Toast the seeds in a frying pan (skillet) without any fat. Stir throughout to ensure they do not burn. Allow to cool a little.
2. Mix with nutritional yeast and rock salt.
3. Freeze or store in an airtight container.

DUKKAH

The aromas in the kitchen when toasting the spices for this Egyptian seed and nut mixture are wonderful. Dukkah is good on salads, boiled vegetables and grilled halloumi, or as a dip with olive oil. This is the basic recipe, which can be mixed with black pepper, chilli flakes, paprika or finely zested orange for a little extra spice in your life.

**MAKES APPROXIMATELY 400 G
(14 OZ/3 CUPS)**

100 g (3½ oz/¾ cup) hazelnuts

100 g (3½ oz/⅔ cup) sesame seeds

2 tablespoons coriander seeds

1 tablespoon cumin seeds

1 tablespoon fennel seeds

rock salt

1. Toast the nuts and seeds in a dry frying pan (skillet) without any fat. Leave them to cool and either blend them or chop them roughly.
2. Toast the spices in the same frying pan without any fat.
3. Mix the nuts, seeds, spices and rock salt. Store in an airtight container.

VEGESAN

Lovely nut sprinkles that are reminiscent of Parmesan, hence the name. The sprinkles are good on everything from pizza and pasta to popcorn, so you may as well make a big batch and store it in an airtight container.

MAKES APPROXIMATELY 300 G
(10½ OZ/2 CUPS)

200 g (7 oz/1⅓ cup)
unsalted cashews

3 tablespoons
nutritional yeast

2 teaspoons onion powder

½ teaspoon salt

1. Mix all the ingredients in a food processor into a fine powder.

FURIKAKE

Sweet and salty Japanese seed mixture that is great on everything from noodles to egg sandwiches. The original contains bonito – smoked tuna fish flakes – which can be replaced with smoked salt. Give it a boost with a few tablespoons of healthy nutritional yeast.

MAKES APPROXIMATELY 200 G (7 OZ)

2 nori sheets (seaweed)

3 tablespoons flaxseeds

3 tablespoons white
sesame seeds

2 tablespoons black
sesame seeds

1 teaspoon rock salt
or smoked salt

pinch of sugar

1. Roast the nori sheets using a burner (the kind used for crème brulée), a gas burner or in the oven. Crumble them finely, either by hand or using a food processor, once they have cooled a little.
2. Toast the seeds in a dry frying pan (skillet) while stirring them.
3. Mix the seeds with the nori, sprinkle in the salt and season with sugar.

TACO SEASONING

The perfect taco seasoning without any sugar. If you want the seasoning to be more like those you can buy, you should add dextrose. Coffee gives a richer flavour and cayenne peppers give heat. Make a big batch for your Friday night parties.

MAKES APPROXIMATELY 100 G
(3½ OZ)

3 tablespoons ancho
chilli powder

2 tablespoons ground cumin

1 tablespoon ground coriander

2 teaspoons oregano

2 teaspoons paprika

1 teaspoon salt

1. Mix all the ingredients and store in an airtight container.

INDEX

WATERFORD CITY AND COUNTY LIBRARIES WITHDRAWN

V = *Vegan Recipe*   **L** = *Leftover dish*

Thank you!

Susanna. Thank you for all the right words and patience. Books don't become beautiful without beautiful design. Thank you, Lukas.

Thanks to Alexandra for your guidance and faith. This gets you a long way.

Since I promised to stop calling you Lennart, I'll do that now. Thank you, Lelle – you are an incredible photographer.

You are my rock, Marta. Dziękuję bardzo.

Mum and Dad. Thank you for making me, and for making me the person I am. And thanks for also having the good taste to arrange for me to have sisters. You're all amazing.

Eje and Sami. Thank you for enriching my life with meatballs, music and love. It would have been very dull without you.

Matti. Thank you for being my guinea pig, helping with the dishes and your patience. Love you.